THE RIGHT WAY
TO
KEEP HAMSTERS

THE RIGHT WAY TO KEEP HAMSTERS

Roy Robinson and David Baglin

RIGHT WAY

CONTENTS

LIST OF ILLUSTRATIONS

FOREWORD

The hobby of keeping small pets has always been a fascinating one for children, and, it may be said, for a large number of adults. Moreover, within recent years, there has been a marked increase of interest in pets of all kinds. This is due to the encouragement of pet keeping in schools and the wider variety of animals now available in pet shops.

Small pets have an appeal of their very own and, more particularly for modern living, a great many advantages. They are not expensive to keep, they do not take up much room and their diet is simple. Proprietary basic foods are easily obtainable from pet shops and supermarkets which can be supplemented by table scraps and left-overs.

Gone too are unsightly wooden boxes. In their place is a range of hygienic plastic and metal cages and tanks in bright colours which may be brought into the living room without being an eyesore. This is ideal for people living in a flat.

Anyone who is away from home all day will find that a hamster can be a most convenient pet. There is no reason why pet rodents should not be as acceptable as canaries or budgerigars. They can give just as much pleasure and, of course, the two kinds of pet should be regarded as complementary, certainly not as competitive.

Just why the hamster has become one of the popular pets of modern times is really not hard to understand. It is small and easy to keep, does not require expensive or uncommon food and its endearing behaviour soon wins over those people who would look upon the little chap as "just another rodent". Another feature that makes hamsters so popular is that they have a most attractive appearance. Long-haired Syrian hamsters especially look like small living teddy bears. Hamsters are also scrupulously clean, constantly grooming and washing themselves after periods of activity. Being native to a semi-desert habitat in the wild, they drink very little and therefore keep their cages quite dry and odour free.

1

DIFFERENT HAMSTER SPECIES

All animals are classified by zoologists into species. A species is a group of animals which interbreed freely, have the same general characteristics, feed on the same food and live in the same surroundings. Some species may occur widely (as is evidently true for the Common hamster) or be restricted to a small area (as seems to be the case for the Golden or Syrian hamster).

There are a number of species of hamster (at least 27 species or more) and only those which are of special interest will be briefly described. Some of these occasionally find their way into pet shops, especially those outlets which deal in the more exotic animals. All of the hamsters are interesting little creatures, although only a few have captured the affections of pet lovers. All of the species are burrowing rodents, inhabiting different regions of Europe and Asia.

The Common or European Hamster
The Common or European hamster (*Cricetus cricetus*) may well be the largest of the various

species. It is about the size of a rat, but with a short tail. Fur colour is grey-brown on the back, with white marks on the cheeks and chest. The belly fur is black. It has distensible cheek pouches which are used to carry food back to its burrow. It is common in central Europe and parts of Russia. The animal is an agricultural pest in Europe, eating large quantities of grain and destroying crops. It is rarely bred in captivity, being too big and vicious.

The Chinese Hamster
The Chinese hamster (*Cricetulus griseus*) is one of the smaller forms and classified as a Dwarf Hamster. In size, it is about 7–10cm (3–4 inches long) with a tail of about 1.5cm (half an inch). It is from a sub-species of hamster known as the "rat-like" hamster. Colour is light grey-brown to chestnut on the back, with an obvious dark stripe down the spine and creamy fur on the stomach. There are the usual cheek pouches for collecting food. See fig. 14 on page 0. It occurs in China and Mongolia. This species is occasionally sold in pet shops, but has never become popular as it is a little too "mouse-like" in colour and size. They also tend to be very reclusive, shying away under bedding or in nest boxes.

The Migratory Hamster
The Migratory hamster (*Cricetulus Migratorius*) is another Dwarf hamster, scarcely any larger than

the Chinese and rather similar. The colour is much the same but lacking the spinal stripe. It is found in southern Russia and Asia Minor. The species is bred in captivity, but has failed to catch on.

The Russian or Djungarian Hamster

Several species of Russian or Djungarian hamsters have quite recently been bred in captivity. These are the **Campbell's Russian hamster** (*Phodopus Sungoris Campbelli*), which came onto the pet market in the late 1960s, the **Winter White Russian hamster** (*Phodopus Sungoris Sungoris*), which was introduced in the mid 1970s (see fig. 13 on page 105), and the **Roborovski Russian hamster** (*Phodopus Roborovski*) which was imported into the UK in the early 1990s.

All three of these species are quite small, only about 3.5–7cm (1.5–3 inches) long, with Roborovskis being the smallest, and are classified as Dwarf Hamsters.

In the wild, Campbell's and Winter Whites are brownish grey with a darker, almost black, stripe along the spine. They have three arches along each flank of a slightly paler shade and light-coloured belly fur. The Roborovski is a pale sandy-gold colour with no spinal stripe, but a white throat, belly, arches and eyebrows instead.

The tail is short for all three species and they have pouches, but these do not appear to be used as freely as other hamsters. They are found in Siberia, Manchuria and northern areas of China. (See also Chapter 9.)

The Mouse-like Hamster

The Mouse-like hamster (*Calomyscus Bailwardi*), which originates from the dry mountains of Afghanistan, is aptly named as it does not resemble a hamster at all. It has a tail longer than its own body length and no cheek pouches. They make their nests in rocky cracks which they line with dry grasses and sheep's wool. They are quite social and can be found in several zoos in Great Britain.

The Korean Grey Hamster

The Korean Grey hamster (*Cricetulus triton*) is one of the larger species. It is about 20cm (8 inches) in length and has a larger tail than most. The colour is mousy-grey with a light belly. It has large cheek pouches and occurs in China and Korea.

It is doubtful if this hamster is bred in captivity but it is worth mentioning because of stories about its remarkable feats of hoarding. (The word "hamster" comes from the German verb "hamstern" which means "to hoard".) "Granaries" have been located several feet under the ground and containing a bushel or more of grain (36.4 litres) stored by the hamsters. During periods of famine, Chinese peasants have survived by digging up the grain.

The Syrian or Golden Hamster

The hamster of the pet shops is the Syrian or Golden hamster (*Mesocricetus auratus*), as shown in fig. 1. It is one of the medium-sized species

Fig. 1. Golden hamster pouching a tasty tit-bit.

being about 12–15cm (5–6 inches) in length when fully grown. The tail is short. The coat colour in the wild is reddish-brown on the back, with two creamy-coloured streaks on the cheeks and shoulders, separated by a black bar. The belly is greyish-cream with a band of reddish-brown and grey across the chest. There are two well-formed cheek pouches which are used to gather up food and nesting material.

The animal occurs in Syria and is thought to be uncommon in the natural state, although this opinion may be due to the fact that it sleeps during the day, only emerging at dusk in search of food.

The Rumanian Hamster
The Rumanian hamster (*Mesocricetus Newtoni*) is a medium-sized animal, about 15cm (6 inches) in length, with a stubby tail. The colour is dark brownish-grey on the back. The stomach is greyish-white except for a blackish chest band. It is found in Rumania and Bulgaria.

This species is similar to the Golden hamster and some authorities have considered that the two are identical. The difference in coat colour was thought to be due to the Rumanian hamster living in the Balkans and the Golden hamster in Syria. However, recent studies have revealed that the two are clearly distinct. It is being bred in captivity and appears to be doing well.

The Caucasian or Georgian Hamster and the Brandt's Hamster
Two other species which are generally similar to the Syrian and Rumanian hamsters in size and colouration are the Caucasian or Georgian hamster (*Mesocricetus Raddei*) and the Brandt's hamster (*Mesocricetus Brandti*). The former, as the name implies, is found in the Caucasus region which lies between the Black Sea and the Caspian Sea. The latter appears to be more widely distributed in the Middle East, ranging from Asia Minor through to

northern Iraq and Iran. There appears to be a complex of species inhabiting the Middle East, all similar to the Syrian hamster, although little is known of their exact relationships.

2

THE ORIGIN AND NATURAL HABITAT OF THE HAMSTER

The Golden, or Syrian, hamster, as it should be correctly referred to, was first recorded in 1839. Examples were kept at London Zoo for around thirty years, from the late 1800s. As the species had not been found again in the wild, it was believed that it had become extinct.

However, a zoologist by the name of Israel Aharoni, on a scientific expedition in Syria, uncovered a mother and a litter of young from a burrow in a field near Aleppo in 1930. Eight of the youngsters were taken to the Hebrew University at Jerusalem. Due to various mishaps, offspring were obtained from only one male and two females. Nevertheless, these thrived in captivity.

The original hamsters were found in April 1930 and the first litter in captivity was born in the following August. It is believed that all of the present day hamsters are descendants of just these three animals. Breeding stock was dispatched to several countries of the world including Britain. This was in 1931, so Britain was one of the first countries to have them.

For many years, the animals were only bred in laboratories, where their nutrition and breeding were studied. Legend has it that a few were given to London Zoo, where they bred successfully and eventually passed into the hands of private breeders.

The Second World War intervened and it was not until 1945 that the hamster was hailed as a novel pet. Since then the delightful little animal has never looked back. Hamsters are now bred by the hundreds of thousands, particularly in Britain and the USA. The first hamster club was formed in the 1940s. The first colour sport (see Chapter 7) was discovered in 1948, followed by many others over the years.

There have been reports that some Syrian hamsters were captured in the wild in the 1980s and eventually found their way onto the pet market but there seems to be no documented proof available on this.

Today there are so many colours that it is difficult for even an expert to keep track of the various forms. However, this is one of the reasons why keeping hamsters is so exciting.

Hamsters in the Wild
The native habitat of many of the species of hamster is a fairly harsh one. The landscape is usually quite rugged and inhospitable to the likes of human beings. Hamsters can be found in quite mountainous terrain, to sub-desert steppes, forests and meadows and scrubby hill land. Temperatures during the day can range from searingly hot to moderately temperate

and can drop to almost freezing at night. Hamsters sleep during the day in cosy nests made of dry grass, within burrows. This protects them from such extremes of temperature.

Their tunnels are either dug from scratch or are improvements made on an uninhabited den left by some other small creature. Within the burrow there are excavated chambers for sleeping, storing food and raising families. The tunnels can be as long as 15 feet (4.5m) and as deep as 6 feet (1.8m).

Hamsters are nocturnal which means that they are most active during the evening and at night. Their thick fur coats over a good layer of body fat, plus constant scurrying around in search of food, keep them warm, even on the coldest of nights.

Wild hamsters are omnivorous foragers which means they will eat almost anything that they can find. Their preferred diet is fallen seeds, nuts, roots, succulent young grass shoots and insects. They will even take scraps of meat if they come across a fresh carcass whilst on their travels.

Hamsters pass two types of droppings. One is dry and pellet-like, while the second is much softer and lighter in colour. Because of the poor nutritional quality of their diet and the fact that it is processed through their bodies quickly, the hamster consumes the soft droppings again and gets every bit of nourishment out of the food it has eaten. Humans may find this unpleasant but it is vital to the animal's well-being. A hamster will travel many miles during the course of a night. Patrolling their home territory and looking for a mate are also high priorities.

3

CHOOSING AND TAMING
A HAMSTER

Choosing a Hamster
Whether you are choosing a pet hamster or a
potential show hamster, you should still consider
the same things before buying your new pet. The
health and temperament of the new animal are
extremely important when making such a choice.

It is natural for a newly weaned baby to panic
when first being handled. This is very normal
behaviour and should stop within a week or so after
arrival at its new home.

Buying from a pet shop
If a pet is all that you require and there are no
hamster breeders locally, a pet shop is a perfectly
acceptable place to get a new hamster. Make sure
that the shop is generally clean and tidy and that
the other animals look well provided for. Ask the
assistant if the animals are in separate sex cages and
see what sort of advice he gives. If the sexes are still
together you may be buying a pregnant female so
beware!

When you have looked in the cages and everything seems to your satisfaction, pick out the hamster that you require and, holding it firmly, check it over to see that it is healthy. A hamster should have no scars or wounds; it should have short, even teeth and be plump and well covered with soft fur and have a clean bottom area. You should also be able to see that its eyes and ears are clean with no tears or mucous when it is awake and moving around in the cage. Look for an animal with bright, bold eyes, a well-groomed coat and lively behaviour. Be wary of animals which are thin, listless and sitting by themselves in a corner. A prominent backbone and a swollen belly are signs of incorrect feeding.

When several hamsters are huddled together, their coats become dishevelled and allowance must be made for this. They should be disturbed, and those which are on their feet quickly, with perky ears and looking around inquisitively for the disturbance, are likely to be the healthiest.

Always buy a hamster where possible between the ages of five to 12 weeks. However, an older animal would still make a nice pet, especially one which has been petted and tamed from a youngster, for these tend to be less nervous of strangers.

In a reputable pet shop, the shopkeeper will give plenty of advice about the right way to keep, handle and feed your new pet and you should go on your way with a new little friend for the next 18 months to three years.

Exhibition quality animals may be bought from pet shops. A hamster with a long face and narrow ears is unlikely to develop into something stunning, so it is wise to choose carefully.

Buying from a breeder
If you would rather buy an unusual colour from a breeder or are looking for a potential show animal, your club secretary should be able to put you in touch with somebody suitable. Once you have contacted the selected person you may have to wait several months for a litter but it should be worth it in the end.

When picking your new hamster from show stock parents, always bear in mind that it is possible that the breeder has kept back the best for himself. This is not always the case though as animals may change through their adolescence and improve greatly on the ones kept back by the breeder.

Occasionally the breeder does not have room to keep any babies back and may ask to keep his lines going by having a baby back from you one day! In some cases with mixed colour litters, the breeder will keep one of one colour and you may get the pick of the others. Quite often a breeder may think that the babies are too alike and won't be able to choose between them.

Hopefully with plenty of good food and loving care your little ball of fluff will turn into a handsome, friendly, lovable friend.

Breeding from your hamster
If your young animal from exhibition stock does not mature into the wonderful show winner that

you expected, having seen its best in prize-winning parents and grandparents, you should not despair. A hamster sadly only has a short life but therefore an early and fast reproductive life. You could choose a suitable mate for your pet, or, if it is a female, a suitable stud male and breed on with it. Good show animals frequently skip a generation and may produce very average offspring, however their descendants may breed good show stock because of their ancestry. So it may only take six months or a year to have your own good lines.

If you have a pet shop bought animal with poor type and colour and decide to breed it with your show lines, you may get marginally better offspring than the original pet shop hamster, but it will take many generations of breeding with good stock to get specimens of a high enough standard to win classes so I would not recommend "wasting" a female from show lines on a poor quality pet shop male if possible. The other way round would be much better as a female has a shorter reproductive period than a male.

It is also worth remembering that no amount of good feeding will turn a rangy sleek type into a rounded cobby fellow favoured by judges.

Taming Your Hamster
A really wild hamster is virtually unknown nowadays. Youngsters may behave as if they are wild, but they usually are just frightened. Even youngsters quickly lose their timidity if they are handled properly from an early age. It is natural for young

animals to show fear, for it helps to protect them from danger.

Once you arrive home with your new pet, it is recommended that the cage be set up for it immediately. Put the box it came in inside the cage, and leave it open for the hamster to come out at its own will. Let the little fellow explore its new home and the new smells for a few hours before trying to handle him.

Most young hamsters are wary of strangers but it is easy to make friends. Do not make sudden movements but always act calmly and gently. Offer tit-bits of food and permit the young hamster to settle down. Sooner or later its curiosity will overcome its fear. If it cowers away when you attempt to pick it up, do not worry. Allow the little fellow to sniff your fingers and it will soon learn that you mean it no harm.

Even humans have to learn to handle hamsters correctly! This soon comes with a little practice. At first, always use two hands in a scooping motion, letting the animal see that you intend to pick it up. Later, when you have confidence in yourself and the hamster is used to being petted, one hand may be used.

This is how it is done: drop the palm of the hand over the animal's body with its head facing away from you. Close your fingers under its tummy and lift gently, yet quickly enough to prevent the animal from scrambling away. Make a tube of your fingers, with only slight but firm pressure on the hamster's body. Do not squeeze. If you hold the hamster too loosely, it will feel unsafe and struggle. Hold it firmly and it will feel secure. As you lift, turn your palm over and towards you, so that the hamster is sitting comfortably in your hand, partly on its back and facing you. Do not hold the animal too long at first, since it may become restless and frightened. By eight to nine weeks of age your hamster should be completely tame.

Hamsters react violently to being teased. Do not poke objects, such as a pencil or a finger, through the wire of the cage. Quite often the little fellow thinks it is something to eat and will bite. Even the tamest of hamsters will do this instinctively.

Another big don't: never disturb a sleeping hamster in its nest. Hamsters sleep very soundly and do not like being wakened by probing fingers. They roll on their backs and show their resentment by biting. A light knock on the side of the cage or scraping of a finger along the wire will usually bring the hamster out to investigate. It is amusing to see them emerge, bleary eyed, yawning and stretching their legs. An angry hamster often advertises the fact by a chattering of the teeth and furious snorting. These are occasions when it is wise to refrain from touching them for a while. Fortunately these "rages" never last for long.

Almost all hamsters enjoy leaving their cages for exercise, particularly in the evening when it is their natural time for a ramble. A large plastic storage box half filled with wood shavings and tubes makes a wonderful playground for a frisky animal. Table tops and sofas are interesting to them too.

However the little chap should never be left on its own. Hamsters have no regard for heights as they cannot perceive depth. They are not always able to land safely on their feet in the way that a cat does should they fall. They often suffer serious injuries from such falls.

Hamsters find the backs of cushions of armchairs and sofas fascinating and have to investigate them. Beware, for such pieces of furniture are notorious hidy-holes when your pet does not want to be put back in its cage. You may find that the cheeky little animal has eaten its way through the back of the chair in no time and escaped onto the floor.

There is also a temptation to allow the animal to run freely on the floor. One must be careful, however, that there are no unsuspected holes or cracks in the skirting or floorboards. If there are, the hamster will surely find them. Escapees usually look for somewhere dark to hide. Should you lose a hamster in this manner, the best policy is to leave its cage on the floor, with the door open, close to the place where it was last seen. Quite often, the little escapee will be found snug in its nest the next morning.

A useful dodge in these circumstances is to set several "traps". These may be deep-sided tins, buckets, boxes, etc., into which the hamster may tumble but not scramble out again. A ramp or stairway should lead up to the lip of the trap. It is surprising how often these simple devices work. A little food should be placed in each trap, not so much to entice the animal but to provide a meal. It would be worthwhile closing all doors and setting a trap in each room. Hamsters are geniuses in finding themselves in "impossible" situations from which they cannot escape. Should your pet go "missing", these places should always be searched immediately.

4

CAGES AND CAGE EQUIPMENT

Hamsters are so adaptable that they may be kept in almost any convenient cage, provided it is soundly constructed and sufficiently large. The generally accepted dimensions for the ideal cage are about 60cm (24 inches) long, 30cm (12 inches) wide and 23cm (9 inches) high. A somewhat smaller cage could be used if the animal is allowed out for a ramble during the evening hours.

Do not fall into the error of thinking that a mouse cage is suitable for a Syrian hamster. Many are too small and the wooden ones are not made robustly enough to stand up to the gnawing of an energetic hamster.

Generally, adult Syrian hamsters must have individual cages. Youngsters can live together until about six to eight weeks of age, then fighting will break out. The females are the worst offenders; they never seem able to live together for long, nor with a male. Males which have grown up together since weaning are the only exception. Even with them, one has to be prepared for a change of heart and a hasty move into separate cages.

Cages

Glass tanks
Glass and plastic tanks are very popular to keep hamsters in. An old aquarium of suitable size makes a very good hamster home. Indeed one which is no longer watertight may be purchased quite reasonably. These can be roomy and are mess- and draught-free.

The glass front would seem to be an advantage since it enables the hamster to be easily observed while it is eating or at play. It is a good idea to paint the other walls white if they are of glass so that the hamster has some privacy.

A wire top should be fitted. It is possible that the hamster may jump or climb out one night or be injured by an inquisitive cat or dog. It is now possible to purchase customised glass tanks especially for small rodents. These have shelves inside them with ladders going up and down to the various levels. They also have fitted wood and mesh lids for good ventilation and air circulation.

Wire mesh cages with plastic bases
The most commonly seen cages in pet shops tend to be rectangular in shape, having plastic bases (rather like large cat litter trays) and a wire mesh cage construction on top of this (see fig. 2). These cages

Fig. 2. Basic cage.

are ideal to keep hamsters in as long as they are large enough. They are very easy to dis-assemble for cleaning and also to maintain in good hygiene as the plastic bases may be washed and dried, quickly and thoroughly. There are many different forms of this sort of cage on the market, some of which have several levels (see fig. 3) providing extra floor space for the hamster and a bigger area to climb on. Multi-floored cages also tend to have several doors for easy access to your hamster. Most wire cages have stainless steel tops but brass ones are also available and these look highly decorative. There is no end of choice for the colours of the cage

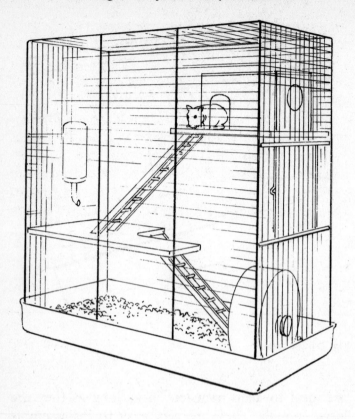

Fig. 3. Basic cage with two levels.

bases. If a nest box is added it will give the hamster somewhere to retire to when it feels it needs some privacy and quiet.

The only downside to wire cages with plastic bases is that quite often the sides of the tray are not so deep as to keep all the cage litter in when the hamster starts digging around inside. This they do frequently, re-arranging their homes or searching for buried food. Many cage bases are only 5cm (2 inches) high and, when a hamster puts his mind to piling up the cage litter in one corner, a great deal of mess can be made all over the shelf or table that the cage is kept on.

One way of overcoming this problem is to make a hamster cage tidy. A cardboard box a little longer and wider than the hamster's cage can be used. Measure the front of the box to the height you require, probably around 3cm (1.5 inches) higher than the height of the cage tray. The back of the tidy should be at least 15cm (6 inches) higher than the top of the cage tray. The sides of the cardboard box should then be cut diagonally from the top of the front to the top of the back. This may then be covered and lined with off-cuts of wallpaper. You will then have a practical solution for keeping mess to a minimum which also serves to keep out draughts and fits in with your decor.

Bird cages, although similar to hamster cages, are usually not suitable. The entrance door is usually too small. They also tend to be a little too high. A hamster could injure itself if it fell from a height of more than 25cm (10 inches) so extra floors would need to be added in the form of sheets of wire mesh. These are easily obtainable from Do It Yourself stores at quite a low cost. Bird cages are often not as robustly made as hamster cages either. The places where the seed cups sit are often of a thinner plastic and are the weak spot where a determined hamster will chew through and escape.

Wire mesh and plastic tray cages may be made at home quite simply and very economically. You will need: a large plastic cat litter tray, a length of welded wire mesh, some wire cutters, a length of thick wire, a bulldog clip and some small split rings rather like the ones used on birds' and rabbits' legs which close together.

Buy the cat litter tray from your local pet shop or garden centre. Welded mesh panels, or rolls with the spacing between the wire 1cm x 1cm (0.5 inch x 0.5 inch) or less, can be purchased from Do It Yourself centres. The metal rings can be bought from hardware stores and pet shops that make their own chinchilla cages.

Cut a strip of mesh at least 20cm (8 inches) wide; it can be wider if you prefer, as this will eventually become the height of the cage. Measure the inside of the litter tray where the wall of the tray meets the bottom. This is where the wire walls will fit. Cut the length of the mesh to the sum of the two longer sides and the two shorter sides. Bend the wire into a rectangular shape, matching the interior of the cat litter tray. This should then have two short walls at either end with two longer ones forming the front and back. Use the metal rings to secure the two ends together. If you cannot obtain these, short lengths of wire can be used to fasten the edges at 4cm (1.5 inch) gaps.

A top should then be cut from another piece of the welded mesh slightly larger than the actual top, with approximately a 2cm (1 inch) overhang on the two short sides and one long side which will become the front of the cage. These three sides should be folded over pointing downwards forming a lip. Fasten the back length of the top of the cage to the

top of the back wall with the metal rings forming
hinges, so that the lid may be lifted and closed.
These rings should be fairly tight-fitting as the
hamster will try and nudge the lid off creating a gap
to escape through at the back, if the rings are too
loose. A bulldog clip at each end will secure the
front of the lid down and keep the hamster inside.

Some coat hanger wire attached 3-4cm (1.5 to
1.75 inches) above the top of the tray in the middle
of each of the short walls at either side should be
bent over at the ends into a v shape. This should
then be hooked around the lip of the tray to stop
the cage being lifted off the base.

Plastic cages
Comparatively recently, brightly coloured plastic
cages have come to the fore. These are a boon in
terms of appearance and hygiene for they too can
be easily cleaned. A number are complete with wire
fronts but many have clear plastic sections for easy
viewing of the inmates.

Of some interest is a system whereby a basic
home or nesting cage can be purchased, which can
be extended by tubes to make a labyrinth of runs
or passages for an inquisitive hamster or other
small rodent to explore. These labyrinth cages (see
fig. 4) are very exciting and attractive to look at
and simulate the natural burrow of a hamster.
They can also be re-assembled in a different layout
to keep the animal inside stimulated. For Dwarf
hamsters they make wonderful homes. Mouse ladders would need to be purchased to enable the

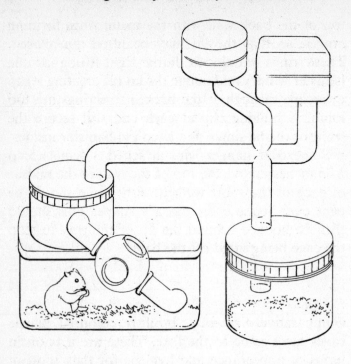

Fig. 4. Labyrinth cage.

smaller hamster to get up and down the vertical tubes. There are, however, a few drawbacks with this style of housing. The tubes connecting the different units can be too small for a large Syrian hamster. You would also need to buy three or four living room units to make enough space for a Syrian to live in comfortably. Each unit costs as much as a regular hamster cage so it could work out expensive. Labyrinth cages have to be taken apart to get to your hamster to pet and handle it as the doors are usually very small.

Single sex groups of Dwarf hamsters will thrive in such a housing system, but, if they are mixed sexes and start breeding, the babies are often born in isolated units away from food and water. They must be fed separately from the adults as they are weaning. A watering system would also need to be set up as babies could easily drown in a water pot placed in their nesting chamber.

Wooden cages
Wooden cages may be used. Wood is a natural product and many people prefer the material. If you intend to make your own cage, wood is invariably the first choice because it is easily worked. Fairly simple box-like cages may be built, either with a wire lid or with a solid top and the front made of wire. A more elaborate cage could be glass-fronted, with either a wire lid or wire-covered ventilation holes at the back or in the top. Clear plastic may be used in place of glass, but this gradually becomes covered in scratches which is a drawback.

A major disadvantage with wooden cages is that the hamsters are persistent gnawers. Any protruding corners are an open invitation to the little beggars and, sooner or later, these will be chewed away. Such corners should either be avoided or be protected with strips of tin. An enterprising hamster will even attack the walls of the cage. Fortunately, however, they need something to get their teeth in initially. Only smooth planed wood should be used; a rough surface is again inviting. Plain wood also seems attractive, compared with painted. Two or even more coats of hard drying paint seem to discourage gnawing.

Gnawing, of course, is perfectly natural and, if the worst comes to the worst, the inside of the cage could always be lined with tin. This is not as difficult as it may sound. Thin sheets of metal can be obtained from tin cans (from tinned fruit and vegetables). The large cans are the best. Slit these open with cutters and carefully straighten the sides. These sheets may be trimmed to size and fastened with small tin-tacks. A coat or two of paint will prevent rusting and also disguise the tin. In fact, painting the cage vastly improves the appearance and is worth doing. White is advisable for the inside while the outside would be of a bright colour to suit your own taste. Be sure to use a non poisonous paint for the interior.

Anyone making a cage for the first time would be advised to have either the top or one side completely removable or have a large door installed. This makes for easier catching of the hamster. After a while, your pet should be so tame that either it does not object to being caught or it scrambles forth of its own accord. But nothing upsets a hamster more than being forcibly pulled through a narrow entrance. It is far better to avoid such a situation by a little forethought in design. From a practical viewpoint, a cage of this type can be cleaned more easily and more thoroughly. The latter is important for elimination of smells and preventing disease.

Plenty of ventilation is important. This is the

main reason for recommending that the top of the cage should be composed of wire. Humidity from the hamster's breath or body can then pass out of the cage instead of collecting as condensation on the "roof". Condensation built up over even a short while may lead to the development of fungal infections within the cage.

Having decided to make the top of wire, or mostly of wire, consider the idea of making it in the form of a lid: a removable lid or one which opens backwards. Wire netting can be used, but if the hamster can reach the netting, it will "worry" it until the strands of wire give way. "Punch-bar" (as used for bird cages) may be used instead or the newer welded meshes. Heavy gauge wire looks unsightly and is not necessary. Spacing between the wire should be about 8mm (³⁄₈ inch) if possible. If the gap is as large as 12mm (¹⁄₂ inch), the hamster can push his nose between the bars and this can lead to rubbing and loss of fur.

Wooden cages are no longer as popular as they were in the 1960s and 1970s since more modern housing systems have been introduced. There is now such a wide choice of lightweight and attractive plastic tray and mesh cages at quite reasonable prices that wooden caging looks outdated. Wooden cages are more of an option to somebody setting up a hamstery in a garden shed or outhouse where an antiquated look is less important and there is a need to keep the cost down. Indeed, solid-sided wooden cages would be an advantage in this situation as they would keep out any draughts.

Metal cages

Metal cages may also be bought at pet shops. They are also not as popular as they used to be since the arrival of plastic and mesh top cages. The advantages to all metal cages are that gnawing is kept in check and that the better cages are well designed and elegant. The bars are chrome while the bodywork is painted in bright colours. Unfortunately as such cages age, the corners can have a tendency to rust with the hamster's urine, unless a toilet jar is used. The larger ones can be heavy to lift and awkward to move around for cleaning and they can also be a little on the cold side if kept in an unheated room. Occasionally metal cages can be on the small side too. One measuring 30cm x 30cm x 20cm (12 x 12 x 8 inches) may be suitable for a mouse, but not for a hamster, unless it is taken out for daily exercise. However, larger cages can be bought and these are preferable. The cost is greater than comparable wooden or other cages though.

One of the reasons why small rodents take so well to captivity is that they do not require large cages or runs. This is due in part to the fact that they are small animals but also partly due to their behaviour. Most rodents not only dig burrows but spend most of their lives in them. A small cage feels like a burrow to a rodent and it helps him feel happier if its design fits in with this idea.

Few people may wish to have too large a cage or are even in the position to have one. If you have a large cage, however, do not leave it empty. Provide a nest or sleeping box as a must, as well as cage "furniture" or "playthings" for the inmates to investigate, run between and climb over. Cubes of wood, tubes of cardboard or empty tin cans, small branches of trees (non poisonous varieties), etc., are suitable furniture. Large empty cages (even with a nest box) can be psychologically stressful to many rodents. Please remember that they are creatures of the undergrowth and like to creep beneath objects and to peer around corners.

Litter and Bedding

The cheapest material for litter is sawdust, small bags of which can be obtained at most pet shops. The sawdust should be devoid of strong odour – except pine which many people find pleasant. Excessively fine or dusty sawdust should be avoided, if possible, since this can cause the hamster to sneeze and may cause other breathing problems. Dry, white sawdust is the best quality but, alas, not always obtainable. However, brownish sawdust serves almost as well, provided it is not damp. Should you be unfortunate enough to buy slightly damp sawdust, either complain to the shop or dry it in an oven before use.

A better option than sawdust, but quite similar and cheap, are wood shavings. These are not so fine as to irritate the eyes and nose of your hamster and are fresh-smelling and pleasant to the eye. The only drawback is that long-haired male Syrian hamsters do occasionally get the curls of wood shavings caught in the long hair around their back ends which quickly get knotted up. So you may need to groom your hamster a little more frequently if you use this as cage litter.

Other materials are peat and cat litter. Peat is suitable, as long as it is perfectly dry to begin with and you do not object to the colour. Many people prefer the light colour of sawdust. Cat litter is very good, although expensive. It has exceptional moisture-absorbing properties and cages with this material should not require cleaning so often. It also enjoys the reputation of keeping down smells. Wood-based cat litter is especially good as it is less dusty for people with dust allergies. Whatever litter you do decide to have, do not be skimpy with it. It is better to use a little too much, than not enough. Candidly speaking, sawdust is adequate as a rule.

There is a choice of several sorts of bedding, but shredded paper is the most frequently used. It is clean, warm, cheap and easily available. Shredded toilet tissue or kitchen towel is ideal. It is possible to purchase bedding from pet shops that is made of a teabag-like material with which hamsters love to build cosy nests. Shredded newspaper should never be given as the print can come off all over the hamster's fur, making it look dirty and it is also poisonous if ingested.

Small bags of meadow hay are sold by most pet shops. This should smell pleasant – certainly not mouldy or dusty. In fact musty hay should never be used, even if it was fresh when you bought it. Though a natural product, one disadvantage of hay is that it will commence to mould under damp conditions. It is also wise occasionally to lightly spray new bags of hay with a flea spray meant for cats or birds as hay can carry mites which may live on your little pet and cause irritation.

Woodwool used to be quite popular, as it could often be had for the asking at greengrocers. Sadly there are fewer and fewer small greengrocer shops around due to large supermarket chains opening up nationwide, and nowadays fruit and vegetables are most frequently packed in polystyrene. Only the softest woodwool should be used if you can still get it. The type used to pack peaches is usually of a fine soft quality. Another useful bedding material which sometimes can be obtained is medicated and shredded parchment.

Hamsters will construct comfortable nests with all of these materials. A good-sized nest is vital for your hamster's comfort and warmth. The little fellows also require privacy and quiet on occasion, so where better to go and hide away than under a big mound of nesting material?

Fluffy bedding which is like cotton wool is still seen in pet shops but should never be used. It is marketed as being "safe" for all small rodents. However, it has been shown that the fibres are actually quite tough and do not break down quickly enough if the animal swallows it. It then gets caught in the gut and kills the animal. Baby hamsters have also had this type of bedding wrapped so tightly around their limbs that the blood supply was cut off and the limb became useless.

Another material that should not be used as bedding is straw. This is rather sharp and can injure the eyes and delicate lining of the hamster's cheek pouches.

Cleaning

One of the aspects you should consider at the onset is whether the cage can be cleaned easily and thoroughly. This is sound advice whether you intend to make your own cage or to buy one. Hamsters do not like being dirty or to live in dirty cages. Make cage cleaning a regular feature of the care of your pet. Weekly cleaning is normally sufficient, depending on the size of the cage. Small cages require more frequent cleaning than large – that is obvious. A mother with a litter will require more frequent attention, especially during the third week of nursing. It is wise not to disturb a hamster with young babies more than necessary. Clean the cage a few days before the litter is expected, then leave for a fortnight if possible.

Very often a corner of the cage may be used as a lavatory and, if the cage is not particularly dirty, the wet sawdust can be removed and the remainder of the nest left undisturbed. However, about once a month, the whole cage should be cleaned. A small wall-scraper is a useful tool for the purpose.

A lavatory, made from a large, glass jar will help to keep cleaning of the cage to a minimum. If wet sawdust from the toilet corner is put into the jar when the jar is introduced to the cage, a hamster will soon learn that this is to be its toilet. The jar can then be emptied and rinsed through daily without having to disturb the rest of the cage too much.

Always check the food store for mouldy items. A well-fed hamster will not eat sour food which becomes smelly if left. Any damp bedding should be taken away (this applies particularly to hay) but do try to put back at least some of the nest material as this encourages the hamster to feel that it has returned safely to its burrow.

Cage Equipment

Various playthings are advocated for hamsters. Exercise wheels, in principle, are a good idea and some hamsters take to them with alacrity. However, wheels which are made for mice are too small for hamsters. If the diameter is small, the animal cannot get inside to use it properly, and, if there is a central spindle, the fur may be rubbed. The solid wheel type with ribs for foot-holds seems to be preferred to the type with wire rungs. The hamster seems to tread these latter rather gingerly but scampers vigorously in the solid wheels.

Hamster balls may also be used for exercising your pet and as a safe way of him exploring the home. As long as a few rules are followed, the hamster will soon get used to and enjoy scampering around in one. Always ensure the ball is on the floor only. Never leave the hamster unsupervised, just in case the ball gets lodged or falls down into somewhere perilous. Never leave the hamster in a ball alone with small children or dogs that may think that it is a toy for them and may be tempted to kick the ball around. Only let your pet run around for a maximum of twenty minutes. A track system is available that can be put together quickly around the room so that the animal can only follow that around and be left unsupervised, quite safely.

Toys or furniture are another matter. Hamsters

(and other rodents) are inquisitive creatures and cannot resist investigating and playing with new objects. These should always be given and changed frequently since novelty is the main attraction. A new toy is played with but an old one becomes part of the surroundings. All sorts of things may be toys. Cardboard tubes or small tin cans (with the ends removed and smoothed down) can be used as tunnels and will afford hours of amusement.

Pieces of odd-shaped wood are useful because these will be chewed and this helps to keep the teeth in good condition. Large branches of fruit trees or other non-poisonous trees are excellent for hamsters to climb on and chew too. It is best to give natural, wooden objects, rather than plastic, and unpainted rather than painted. The number of toys which can be given is limited by the size of the cage. A small cage will only take a few, whereas a large cage gives more scope. In fact, a very large cage should not be left empty but be deliberately filled with furniture, for reasons explained earlier.

Occasionally you may need to transport your pet to some other location, perhaps to the vet or to a show. A transparent plastic carrying box is ideal for this purpose. They are inexpensive, lightweight and well ventilated. They also come in a range of different sizes depending on the species that needs to be carried.

5

FEEDING

It has rightly been said that hamsters will eat anything – well, almost anything. Most rodents are nibblers and the hamster is no exception. Leave a hamster on a table, say, with a mixed variety of food and watch its behaviour. It will pouch quite a lot but it is especially interesting to see the way it tastes or samples the various items. The little fellow will scurry from one bit of food to the next, testing this and tasting that. It will only occasionally settle down to steady munching.

Pouching is different. Finding something which it likes, a hamster will stuff its pouches to the full, run off to its nest, empty its pouches and return for a refill. In its nest, the hamster will eat steadily something it fancies, but outside there is the tendency to nibble. If you observe carefully, it will nibble many items which are not edible. In this way, the animal learns which things are eatable and which are not. It also ensures that a wide variety of different foods are consumed. This is beneficial because it helps to provide a balanced diet and because, if he should eat something which disagrees with him, insufficient amounts will be consumed to cause serious illness. A "balanced diet" is simply a collection of foods which gives the hamster all it requires for rapid and healthy growth.

No skill is required in feeding hamsters if one keeps to the principle of feeding as varied a diet as possible. People who tend to treat the animal as a "scavenger", feeding scraps and left-overs from the table as well as a certain amount of specially pre-pared hamster mix, are on the right lines. They may have to guard against the possibility of over doing it occasionally because they happen to have rather a lot of a certain waste food. Almost all human foods are suitable for hamsters and, because we like a varied diet, it is usually possible to see to it that the pet hamster is well provided. There is also the fact that feeding household scraps is inexpensive!

It is only necessary to feed hamsters once a day. This may be at any time, but during the evening is most convenient – both to the hamster and its owner. If you make a practice of feeding about the same time, the hamster soon learns when grub is on the way and waits eagerly. Tit-bits are appreciated at any time and hamsters like to receive them as much as you like to give them. A particularly tasty tit-bit may induce the hamster to eat it on the spot, but do not be surprised if the greedy animal pouches it and continues to sit up for more.

Suitable food for hamsters (and most other rodents) falls naturally into three groups. Dry food: grains and cereals, whole grains (wheat, oats, sun-flower, mixed bird seeds, etc.) and meals (bran, middling, etc.). Various made up diets, including complete diets such as puppy meal, kitten meal, dry complete dog food and rodent pellets. Green food: fresh leaves (lettuce, cabbage, beans etc.), fruit (apple, melon, pear) and vegetable roots (carrot, swede, etc.). The number of different foods and diets which may be given is large and the best one can do is to indicate those which are the most suitable.

Mealworms are relished by some hamsters and are full of protein. They are sold in pet shops as food for exotic pets such as snakes, lizards and tarantulas. Only one or two per week should be given.

There is quite a lot of faddism in feeding, but the following rules will ensure that your pet will come to no harm. Firstly, feed a varied diet; secondly, do not feed anything which you would not eat yourself. The second rule does not apply to specially formulated diets, of course, such as rabbit and other rodent pellets, mealworms and complete meals for dogs and cats. You may feel you would not like to eat these. They may taste bad to you, but they are wholesome and hamsters love 'em.

The only foods that are not recommended are spicy foods, sticky foods such as sweets and chocolate which can melt within the pouch and be difficult to remove, and anything containing alcohol.

Grains and Cereals

Hamsters are very fond of sunflower seeds and mixed grains of all descriptions: whole or crushed oats, wheat, shelled peanuts, etc. Many of these can be bought as mixed hamster food, rabbit food or even as bird food. This does away with the bother of buying separate items. Proprietary hamster food is sold either loose or in packets by most pet stores and can be purchased in most supermarkets too, another means of buying a mixture in one go.

Mention must be made of the handy rabbit pellet. Most rodents do well on this and the hamster is no exception. The pellet is a formulated diet, made up of cereals, concentrates and vitamins. In more recent times other rodent pellets similar to the complete diet pellets fed to laboratory animals have become available on the pet market. These are specifically for hamsters, rats, mice and gerbils and are a balanced diet in themselves. It is not wise to give your pets solely these pellets as they will soon become rather bored with the same thing day in, day out, but give them along with the basic mix of seeds, nuts, grain and dog biscuit. Breakfast cereals, whether dry or in a small bowl with a little milk added, will be eaten with relish by hamsters too and may be fed three or four times a week as a treat and a conditioning food.

Mashes are favoured by some people for hamsters. The contents of these can vary greatly, from mixtures of bran, middling and maize with water added, to boiled potatoes and cabbage, dried off with bran or dried breadcrumbs. All mashes should be slightly on the dry side; a crumbly consistency is best, never wet or sloppy. Once mixed, mashes do not keep; hence, only small amounts can be made up at one time. On balance, it is doubtful if mashes are worth the bother for adult hamsters. However, youngsters enjoy mashes, particularly when newly weaned.

The most convenient table scraps are those which are not messy. Waste bread in the form of end slices of loaves, crusts, odd left-overs and the like should never be tipped into the refuse bin if you have a hamster. Stale cake and biscuits are also enjoyed. It is a useful trick to bake fingers or cubes of bread in the oven. For one thing, these keep excellently in an airtight tin and, for another, they are good for the hamster's teeth. Dog biscuits serve the same purpose.

Soaked puppy meal and kitten food are another ideal weaning food for young hamsters. They are a complete food in themselves for cats and dogs and excellent for promoting growth when fed as a supplement to the usual basic dry diet. Dry complete foods formulated for puppies and kittens must always be soaked for a good 15 minutes before being offered to your hamster as they could swell up inside the hamster and cause severe discomfort. This sort of food should only be fed to adult hamsters occasionally as a conditioning food as too much will make the little fellow rather too fat.

Green Food and Roots
Green food should form part of a hamster's diet. In the main, this should consist of green leaves. Outside leaves and trimmings from vegetables are ideal. Cabbage, cauliflower, broccoli, curly kale, lettuce, watercress, celery, spinach and carrot tops may be fed. Greengrocers often have trimmings which may

be had for the asking (politely) if you do not wish to buy. The green leaves of cabbage are better than the white (heart) leaves, although the latter are better than nothing.

Vegetable roots, such as beetroot, carrot, swede and turnip, may be fed. These should be cut into small slices or cubes. Many can be obtained all year and will be especially useful for winter feeding when green leaves are less easy to obtain or may be damaged by frost. Never feed frosty green food or roots – not even those which have thawed. These can usually be recognised by a dark colour and a "pulpy" feel. Frosty food is definitely harmful.

Weeds from the garden should not be overlooked. Common weeds such as dandelion, chickweed, groundsel, sow thistle, dead nettle, yarrow, plantain and shepherd's purse, are relished. Lawn mowings are a valuable food, so long as these are from a regularly mowed lawn so that the hamster receives succulent young shoots, not coarse old grass. It is fun making up "salads" of mixed leaves and roots on a tin lid, and your pet will enjoy sorting through the mixture.

There are a number of weeds which are poisonous and these must be avoided at all costs. Bindweed, bluebells, buttercups, hemlock, nightshade, ragwort, scarlet pimpernel and speedwell are those most likely to be encountered. If you are unsure of any weed, err on the safe side and do not feed it to your hamster.

Hamsters love ripe apples and pears. These should be sliced or cubed, as with roots, so that small pieces can be fed. Large pieces of food will only decay in the cage and may, in fact, become soiled by the hamster's droppings and urine. A good plan is to put aside pieces of vegetable when preparing the dinner or pieces from an apple or pear you may be eating yourself.

Food which can be given as tit-bits need not consist solely of vegetables or fruit. Most rodents are fond of dried foods, such as currants, figs, prunes, raisins and sultanas. Nuts of all types may be given. Those with hard shells should be cracked open and the kernel extracted. Unshelled nuts will be easily accepted, but you are likely to find them stowed away, uneaten. Most hamsters are cunning enough not to spend time laboriously gnawing at a hard shell when there is plenty of other food waiting to be eaten.

Be careful not to overdo the feeding of green food. Green leaves are essentially a bulk food and, as such, would not be sufficiently nutritious for quickly growing young hamsters. For adults, green food is useful for preventing over fatness (excess fat is not harmful in itself but can interfere with breeding) but never feed very wet green food. This appears to be a cause of stomach upsets as the hamster consumes more water than it would normally. If the green food is wet, it should be allowed to dry by being spread out on paper.

At all times, only fresh green food should be provided. Never use green food which has turned yellow with age; particularly the yellowed leaves of cabbage, cauliflower or lettuce, for example. Dirty or mud-splashed green food should not be considered. Also, do not use green food which is known to have been recently sprayed with pesticide.

Hoarding

The hamster is well known for its pronounced hoarding instinct. Most rodents hoard but the hamster is equipped with two special cheek pouches into which the little animal will pack the most amazing items. The purpose of the pouch is to gather food which is then carried back to the nest. This instinct is so strong that the hamster will quickly pouch its food, race over to or into its nest and disgorge. It will do this even if the distance between the food and the nest is merely a few inches.

Rodents differ in their feeding instinct. Mice and rats, for example, will seize a piece of food and run back to the nest and sit there eating it. A rabbit will approach the offered food and stay there eating its fill. A hamster may eat a little of the food it has taken to its nest but it is just as likely to come back and refill its pouch, only settling down to its meal when there is no more food to be had.

The usual place for hoarding is at the back of the nest, but other sites may be chosen, and often are.

The habit of hoarding has its advantages but also some drawbacks. A hamster will draw upon its food store until all is eaten. This is all right if the food store consists of non-perishable food. However, since everything is hoarded, the perishable items will become bad. This means that a watchful eye has to be kept on the store and the perishable items removed before they have decayed too much. This may be done as often as one wishes but certainly at the weekly cage cleaning. The hamster's store should be replaced, but only with sound food.

Water

Hamsters have need for water and a supply should always be on hand. Fortunately water bottles can be bought which are fixed on the outside of the cage. Some cages have small holes to take the drinking spout and, in other cases, the spout is simply inserted through the wire. The nozzle of the spout should not be so low that it makes contact with the sawdust (the water will be drained out through capillary action) nor too high so that the hamster cannot find it. Always keep the bottle well filled (since it is inclined to dribble at the slightest movement when almost empty) and regularly washed (to prevent the growth of green slime). These water bottles are greatly superior to the old fashioned water-pot which is so often filled with sawdust or overturned by the industrious hamster.

Holidays

When the whole family goes on holiday, the tending of pets becomes a problem. With cats and dogs, one solution is to have these boarded with a reputable cattery or kennel. This cannot be so easily arranged for a hamster. Some pet shops are willing to care for pets over holidays, but most are not. It should be realised that it is not only the labour involved, but also the responsibility which deters many shops. The vogue of going on holiday in this country in the family car raises the advantage of taking your pet with you. The average hamster cage is not that large and it should be possible to squeeze it in.

A friendly neighbour may be persuaded to tend your pet, either looking in from time to time, or the cage could be taken to them for safe-keeping. If you have a school chum who has pets of his own, what could be better? At least you will know that the hamster will be in the care of someone who is used to looking after pets. You could offer to feed your friend's pets when he is on holiday. Since he could be in the same predicament as yourself, the offer may be received with enthusiasm.

If the worst comes to the worst, a hamster can usually be left unattended for about a week. The provision of food should not be a difficulty since whatever is given will promptly be hoarded and the little fellow will draw upon this whenever he feels hungry. It is clear that no perishables should be given but the more solid hard food such as seeds, rabbit pellets or baked bread. Not even pieces of carrot or apple should be given since it is doubtful that these would last a week in wholesome condition.

The question of water should be considered. Since the hamster will not be receiving any green food, more than the normal amount of water will be drunk. The number of days should be counted which elapse before the water bottle requires a refill. If this is less than the number of days which you will be away, a second bottle should be obtained. Even if the bottle did last just a week, this is unlikely to be sufficient because of the probability that extra water will be consumed. It is better to err on the safe side and fix another bottle temporarily.

Grooming

Hamsters keep themselves meticulously clean and well groomed and do not need to be washed. If however some sort of accident occurs which means that your hamster becomes dirty and needs to be cleaned up, then there is no problem with washing him. A mild soap should be used on an already wet hamster and rinsed off with warm water. The hamster may then be placed on a towel in a dry bowl, bucket or similar container and dried with a hair dryer on a warm setting for a few minutes. The fur will start to fluff up after a short while. Be careful not to over-heat him. The hamster should then be kept in a warm draught-proof place for a couple of hours until fully dry. If the hamster gets chilled, it could easily catch pneumonia and become very ill quite quickly.

6

BREEDING

Sooner or later, after a little experience with feeding and general care, one's thoughts turn to the subject of breeding. Indeed, why not? For much of the enjoyment of hamster keeping is in the expectation of babies. Young hamsters are just as much fun as adults – more so in the opinion of many people. The only trouble is that they grow up so quickly!

Age for Breeding
Hamsters will breed at a very tender age if allowed, but this is definitely unwise in the case of the female. The young are often born undersized and the mother may be physically incapable of feeding them properly. Only fully grown females should be bred from. A breeding age of between 14 and 16 weeks would be better for the majority. Males may, in fact, be bred from much earlier, around the age of seven or eight weeks, because they do not have the strain of rearing a litter and the act of mating is not harmful. If a male is not sexually mature he will not mate, it is as simple as that.

Mating

Since hamsters have to be housed individually, breeding is not simply a case of leaving the male and female together, as with gerbils or mice for example. The two sexes have to be placed together and the mating supervised. The male is normally always ready for mating but the female is not. She will only accept the attention of the male every fourth day and then only rather late in the evening. This is the heat period, as it is termed, and, while some females will come on heat early in the evening, others do not until quite late. The heat period lasts for most of the night, so the later the mating is attempted, the greater the chances of finding the female "on heat".

The most straightforward method of determining whether or not a female is in heat is by placing her with the male. This may be done on a convenient table top, in an open box, empty pen or, most effectively, in the male's cage. Never put the male in the cage of the female – even females in heat have been known to attack the male because of the intrusion. When the two come together, the male will investigate the female. If the female is ready, she may move about for a few moments in a hesitant sort of way, pursued by the male, and then she will "freeze". This posture is unmistakable: the female will crouch slightly, with head pointed forward, body and hind legs extended and tail pointing upwards. Should she move about excessively but not attack the male, the mating posture can often be induced by lightly tickling the female's back with the tip of a finger nail.

An experienced male will promptly mate the motionless female. This is done by the male climbing on to the back of the female from the rear. Successful matings are shown by the male drawing his body up strongly, followed by an immediate dismount. He will wash himself briskly, perhaps lick the female briefly, and promptly mount her again. This process will be repeated many times, with short intervals of rest. The female will be unmoving unless she is disturbed by a sudden noise. The mating should be permitted to continue for about fifteen to twenty minutes or stopped sooner if either the male loses interest or the female unfreezes and starts to attack the male. A male who has not mated before may mount the female from the front or even from the side but eventually will find the correct position and the mating will proceed smoothly.

If the female is not in heat, she will react vigorously toward the male; prancing around with a high stepping walk, rearing on her hind legs or turning on her side, probably snorting the whole time. She may also press her hind quarters firmly against the floor. A fight will ensue if the male persists in his attentions. The two hamsters should be separated at once. Young males have been known to become shy of mating because they have been savaged by females. Older males will fight back. If you have tried the female early in the evening, she could be re-tried later on, just in case she is one of those which does not come in heat until late. The female should be placed with the male on successive evenings until she eventually accepts the mating.

Failure to Breed

Most female hamsters will accept matings every four days without bother. However, there are exceptions and these may be due to different causes. The most common cause is over-fatness. A well-fed female which has not been bred from until she is six months of age or more has had time to fatten up. Had she been bred from at three and a half months, the fat would have gone on feeding her babies. This is not to say that all young females must be bred from, nor to imply that all females will become over-fat. Not at all; the point is that an older female has had time to accumulate excess fat.

The same thing can happen to a female which has had a litter but not for some months. She too, can become over-fat. One can only persevere with her, day after day. The cereal content of her diet should be reduced (and mash, if fed) and fresh young green leaves substituted. Males can also become over-fat, but this rarely interferes with their mating ability.

The season of the year can modify the heat periods of a female. The short days of autumn may bring about a cessation which can last throughout the whole of the winter. Breeding during the winter months is not always good policy, although, with centrally heated houses, this is not the problem it used to be. The "Winter pause" can sometimes be overcome by exposing the female to electric light as soon as daylight starts to fade. An extra four hours or more may be required, and even this may not be successful. Do not be surprised if you have to wait for the arrival of the longer days of spring before a female becomes ready for breeding.

Another aspect is that a female which has never been bred from may become prematurely sterile. Hamster females can breed until they are about fourteen months of age. An unbred female may become sterile at twelve months, or earlier, due to a combination of over-fatness and attempts to reduce her fat. The act of reducing fatness by semi-starvation is not wise. Yet another cause is that the female is unable to have any heat periods. This form of infertility, however, is rare, but could be the reason for persistent refusal to mate when all other possibilities are excluded.

All of the above explanations for a female not coming into heat assume that the animal is in good condition – too good if fatness is the cause. A female may not accept the male because she is out of condition or thin. It is not fair to breed from a thin female and it has been assumed that you would not attempt to do so.

Not all matings necessarily result in a litter. Should the stomach of the female not be swollen by the twelfth day of pregnancy, this may indicate either a small litter or that the mating has not been success-ful. One can wait until the seventeenth or eighteenth day, when the arrival or non-arrival of a litter will decide the issue. However, if you are anxious for a litter, the female can be tried daily with the male. If the mating has failed, the female nearly always comes into heat again about the twelfth to four-teenth day and, thus, a few days' delay can be saved.

The gestation period – the time between mating and birth of young – is sixteen days; one of the shortest periods among mammals. By about ten days, the mother-to-be should be swelling in the tummy and one can tell if she is pregnant or not. By fifteen days, females which are due to have large litters are almost like walking tennis balls. This does not inconvenience them, and it is surprising how agile they can be. The average size of a litter is between six to eight babies, but a large healthy female may have as many as sixteen (even more, on rare occasions).

Proud owners are apt to boast how their pet has brought up a fine litter of fourteen or more young. It is certainly an achievement, but one which imposes a considerable strain on the female and it may be wondered if it is always wise. A new-born litter may be briefly examined by removing the mother from the cage and opening the top of the nest with a ball-pen or similar object. The babies may be roughly counted. Most females can rear up to ten young comfortably. Over this number you should consider reducing the litter. If you can arrange it, the smallest babies should be painlessly destroyed by a vet. Many mothers with large litters do, in fact, eat a few babies. This is nature's way of taking care of excess numbers.

Be careful how you handle a pregnant female. Accidents do happen, and a fall could result in the regrettable loss of the unborn babies, and perhaps the mother. In fact, the female should be left alone for the last few days of pregnancy. She will be busy making a cosy nest for her young and you can help by providing plenty of soft paper bedding or wood-wool. The cage should be cleaned out prior to the arrival of the litter, since it is advisable not to disturb the female more than absolutely necessary for the next fortnight. These precautions are not so important if you have made a fuss of your pet and she is used to you. But beware of allowing strangers to handle her and, particularly, to touch the young.

The babies are born naked and pink in colour, with their eye-lids tightly sealed. They also have teeth which is unusual for baby rodents. Depending on the variety, the skin darkens with pigment, within a few days for the golden, dark grey, black and other dark-coated colours, longer or not so intensely for others. The skin of the albino and cream never darkens. The eyes open by about the twelfth day and by this time the little toddlers will be venturing from the nest. Their walk is very unsteady and wobbly. The mother is often beside herself on these days, running around, picking up her wandering babies and trying to bundle them back into the nest. No sooner has she turned her back than they are out again!

The female will eat voraciously while she is suckling and she should be given all that she needs. The young begin eating before they leave the nest, obtaining nourishment from the food which the mother takes back to the nest. As soon as they are able to toddle around on their own, the food consumption will increase, so be careful not to be caught napping. Be lavish, for it is impossible to overfeed either the mother or the young at this time. The cage will require frequent cleaning and uneaten food can be removed. Mashes made with milk, bread or porridge soaked in milk, or soaked puppy meal, should be given as a supplement for the mother and young, from as soon as the litter are born. This should continue during the weaning stage, even though they are capable of eating the same food as the mother. Baby hamsters, which are regularly fed on soft food supplements until maturity, grow into larger, stronger adults.

Weaning (separating the litter from the mother)
The young hamsters are frisky and well able to look after themselves by three weeks of age. They can be weaned at this time, although many people delay weaning to four weeks. However, they should not be left with the mother too long because she may turn on them. This may seem curious, but hamsters are solitary creatures and the mother seems to feel that she has done her bit and it is time for the young to fend for themselves. The youngsters themselves will live together happily until about six to eight weeks before fighting becomes serious. However, fighting could start sooner and one must be on the alert.

Rearing a litter places a strain on a female and it is not surprising that she often loses weight and becomes thin. She may do this in spite of a satisfactory diet and extra food. It is quite natural and simply a reflection of the fact that most of the food is passed on to the babies as milk. Once the young are weaned, the female should rapidly regain her former condition. She should not be re-mated too soon after the weaning of the young. It is better to wait until the female has regained herself. Four to six weeks ought to be sufficient, but be guided by the animal's condition rather than by the calendar. The other side of the coin is that if you wait too long before deciding to have another litter, the female may become too fat for easy breeding.

Sexing

Young hamsters of mixed sexes should not be left together for long, otherwise unexpected litters will make an appearance. The separation must be done before six weeks or earlier if possible. Juvenile hamsters are more difficult to sex than adults. The simplest method is direct examination of the sex organs. The hamster should be upturned in the palm of the hand. In the female, two small openings (vulva and anus), sited just in front of the tail, can be seen, almost touching, with no hair in between, whereas, in the male, there is only one opening (the anus) but a small pimple a quarter of an inch or so from the anus and separated by hair. In addition, when the animal squirms in the hand, two ball-like glands can often be seen moving under the skin on each side of the vent in the male.

The female has fourteen nipples in two rows of seven down each side of the stomach. These can easily be seen as prominent "teat spots" in the very young hamster, but are less obvious as the fur grows. They can still be seen, however, in older animals by gently blowing apart the hair. Nipples are completely absent in the male and this method of distinguishing the sexes is reasonably reliable. As the hamster becomes older, the sex differences become more pronounced. The female always has a rounded appearance at the rear, while the tail region in the male becomes more and more elongated as the male sex glands develop into two definite pouches.

7

VARIETIES
AND EXHIBITING

The original colouring of the hamster is the familiar golden brown. This is the wild hamster and, for some fifteen years after domestication, was the only known colour. However, nature produces variations in the form of "sports", or "mutants" to use the correct word. No-one knows when, where or what form these may take, except that they do occur at an extremely low frequency. This is how the many colour and fur varieties of not only the hamster but all domestic pets have originated.

It is even more fascinating that, when several mutants are known, these may be combined with each other to produce new series of colours, many of them novel and some exceedingly beautiful. Hamster breeders have selectively bred and preserved these colours so that pet lovers who appreciate beauty can enjoy them too. No attempt can be made to describe all of the possible colours. There are many which differ slightly from one another and these are not recognised by hamster clubs.

Colour Varieties

Hamsters can be found in one colour all over and these are known as "selfs". Animals with a main body colour plus head markings and/or ticking (which will be explained in more detail later in this chapter) of another colour are known as "marked" or "agouti" varieties.

One of the earliest colours to appear was the **Black-eyed Cream** and that variety still ranks among the most popular. The eyes and ears are dark and the body fur is a rich peachy yellow. The colour occurs with red eyes – the **Red-eyed Cream**. The fur colour is slightly pinker, while the ears are brownish rather than black.

One of the most vivid colours (so far at least) is the **Cinnamon** hamster (see fig. 5). The top fur is a bright, rich cinnamon-orange, whilst the under-coat is a deep slate-blue. It has claret-red eyes and light grey-brown ears. There is only one other variety which

Fig. 5. Cinnamon hamster, one of the brightest-coloured varieties.

surpasses it for magnificence of colour. This is not another colour but the combination of **Cinnamon with Satin** (see under Coat Varieties, page 82). A rich orange-brown variety which on some occasions has been mistaken for a Cinnamon is the **Rust** or **Guinea Gold**. The coat is more brown than the Cinnamon and in good exhibition stock it is evenly covered with very dark, almost black, ticking. The under-colour is brownish-grey and the eyes are very dark brown, almost black. It is responsible for producing the **Chocolate** when combined with either the Cream and Umbrous genes or with the Black gene.

Sable is a colour which is a combination of Cream and Umbrous. The top colour is almost black with cream showing through underneath. The fur immediately around the eyes is a pale cream. The **Umbrous** gene is a sooting gene which gives a greyish cast over colours such as Golden, Cinnamon and Rust. When combined with Cream, the Umbrous gene can give a range of pleasant self colours such as **Mink**, which is a medium shade of brown with a tinge of orange, and **Copper**, which is a very orangey/coppery shade of brown.

When Sable and Silver Grey are combined, a colour called **Silver Sable** will be produced. This is very much like a Sable, having a blackish top colour, however, the under-colour and eye circles become a bright silvery-white and give a startlingly attractive appearance.

The name of the **Black-eyed White** accurately describes the variety. In the ideal animal, the eyes and ears are dark and the coat is pure white. When bred through the White Belly gene (see also Chapter

8, page 99) crossed with Cream, many have a yellow tinge in the coat, particularly on the forehead. This is a fault. They may also have mottled ears which is also undesirable. However, when the Silver Grey gene is crossed with Cream, an absolutely pure white animal is produced which has no such yellow tinge to the coat. The ears tend to be uniformly dark from such a genetic combination. The variety is not common, but still has its adherents.

Two forms of albino hamster are known. The first is the **Dark-eared Albino**. As the name implies, the ears are darkly pigmented. The young animal of a few weeks of age has pink ears, the ears darkening from about four to five weeks. The eyes are red and the fur is snowy white. It is more correctly known as the Dark-eared White nowadays, not being a true albino on account of the pigment on the ears and occasionally on the genitals. At present it is the closest gene to the Himalayan/Siamese gene in other rodents and cats, but sadly the colour is restricted to

Fig. 6. Albino variety of hamster.

only the ears and does not continue as far as a face mask or have colour on the legs. The other form is the **Pale-eared Albino**. In this, the ears are flesh-coloured and the eyes are bright, clear pink. The pink eyes and ears, together with the white coat, make the variety comparable to the albino of the mouse and other rodents. It can be, in fact, the combination of the Dark-eared White and the Cinnamon genes and therefore once again, not a true albino.

The **Yellow** might be mistaken at first sight for a Black-eyed Cream. Both the eyes and ears are dark but the coat is deeper in colour than the Black-eyed Cream and is covered with dark guard hairs (or ticking), giving a duskier appearance. There are also noticeable head markings on a Yellow, both on the cheeks in the form of flashes, and around the skull in the form of a sort of cap. The flashes are a band of concentrated ticking, forming a bar going across the cheeks just above an area around the collar which is paler in colour and has no ticking. The areas around the collar are known as the crescents. These dark guard hairs are completely lacking in the cream and make identification of the Yellow easy.

The **Honey** is a form of Yellow but with red eyes and lighter coloured ears. It is the genetic combination of Yellow and Cinnamon. The coat colour is a more orange shade than yellow, without dark guard hairs. Light-coloured guard hairs are sometimes present, but have to be searched for carefully to be noticed. The colour is deeper than the Red-eyed Cream to which it has some resemblance. This variety also possesses faint head markings like the Yellow.

The **Black** is a wonderful variety; the colour is

solid black with a deep blue under-colour. It may also have variable white patches on the stomach. Ideally these should be as small as possible.

The **Chocolate** is another self variety and comes in two forms. One is from Rust and Black. It should be a deep chocolate-brown with a slightly grey-brown under-colour, whereas Chocolate from Sable and Rust, which is the other form, is a more medium shade of chocolate-brown and has pale eye rings.

A pretty variety is the **Dove**. This is a combination of Black and Cinnamon. The coat is a softly toned dove-grey, as evenly coloured as possible with little white underneath. Whereas the Black and Chocolate have dark eyes, the Dove has dark red eyes.

The **Tortoiseshell** is a curious-looking hamster. The coat is a mixture of yellow and coloured patches, most often Golden or Black, usually inter-mingled but sometimes separated into separate patches. The banded (see later) Tortoiseshell, or **Tortoiseshell and White** as it is known, is superior to the ordinary Tortoiseshell in this latter respect because the presence of the white pattern encour-ages the separation of the yellow and the coloured areas. This produces a most attractive variety.

The Golden and Black are not the only Tortoise-shells to be bred. It is possible to breed them in all of the marked varieties (colours which have head mark-ings i.e. flashes and crescents) such as Lilac (see later), Dark Grey (see later), Rust and Cinnamon Tortoiseshell, etc., and many of the self varieties such as Dove and Chocolate Tortoiseshell. The yellow areas of the coat remain, varying in shade depending on the colour used, but these are combined with the

colours listed above. All of these varieties may have
the banded pattern which makes them all the more
fascinating. The art of breeding the varieties is to
have the contrast between the yellow and coloured
areas as great as possible. It is strange, however, that
in the Cream-related colours it is not possible to
breed a Tortoiseshell. The yellow patching is masked
by such colours and you will never see a Sable, Mink
or Copper Tortoiseshell. By the way, the Tortoise-
shells are female for the same biological reason that
Tortoiseshell cats (with rare exceptions) are female.

Three varieties known as "Greys" are bred: the
Light Grey, with a coat colour of light smoky grey,
shot through with creamy beige; the **Dark Grey**,
with a dark grey coat and a band of light pearl-grey
to the hairs which may be seen when the coat is
blown apart; lastly, the **Silver Grey**, where the coat
is a bright silvery-grey. The Greys are engendered
by deficiency of yellow pigment. The Light Grey
has a little, the Dark Grey even less and the Silver
Grey has none at all. The eyes and ears are dark for
all the Greys.

Some of the rarer colours are most attractive. The
Beige and **Lilac** are a soft, pale grey with a pinkish
tone to the coat. The Beige is sprinkled with dark
brown guard hairs which it inherits from Rust and
Dark Grey, and the eyes are dark brown, whereas
the lilac has no guard hairs and claret-red eyes. This
it inherits from its Cinnamon ancestors. Both Beige
and Lilac have grey-brown ears. The **Smoke Pearl** is
a light pearly ivory grey, evenly sprinkled through
with slate-grey guard hairs. The eyes are black and
the ears are dark grey, almost black. This is a

combination of Dark Grey and Yellow. A red-eyed form of smoke pearl called **Lilac Pearl** is known, with brown guard hairs and grey-brown ears. It is similar to Lilac but much paler. **Blonde** is a very pale creamy colour. It has a mask of orange and a light grey-brown under-colour. This can be bred from Light Grey and Cinnamon or Silver Grey and Cinnamon. **Ivory** which can sometimes be confused with Blonde is another pale creamy colour. It is lighter, however, than Blonde, and has no under-colour. This colour can be bred from any of the three Greys as mentioned before, combined with Cream. There is a black-eyed and a red-eyed form which both have the same colour fur; the black-eyed having dark grey ears and the red-eyed having pale grey-brown ears.

White Marked Varieties

The **White Band** (see fig. 7) has a belt of white encircling the midriff. Ideally, the band should be of even width all round the body and not broken by a spinal stripe of coloured fur, as so many are. The coloured parts of the coat may be Golden, Cream, Cinnamon, Grey to name the most usual. Therefore to describe a White Band fully, the colour must also be given, such as Cream White band for a Cream hamster with a band of white. There is a tendency nowadays to omit the word white, since this has been taken for granted. Great favourites among hamster lovers are the Cinnamon Band, the bright orange cinnamon colour making a powerful contrast to the white of the band, and the

Fig. 7. White Band hamster nibbling a piece of biscuit.

Black Band with an even more striking contrast.

The **Piebald** was the first colour sport to occur, about 1945 in the USA. The variety has white and coloured patches of fur intermingled all over the body. The white areas are the novelty, and these can vary from a coloured hamster with white marks on the head, stomach and here-and-there on the body, to an almost white animal with coloured spots on the head and body. As with the Band, the coloured parts may be of any colour. However this variety is extremely rare if not extinct nowadays. This is partially due to the fact that the females do not make good mothers and are more likely to eat or desert their young if not given more privacy than a non-Piebald female. A lack of popularity and accurate record keeping in the mid 1980s within the hamster fancy meant that hamsters

Fig. 8. Golden Piebald hamster.

carrying Piebald were not bred together and thus the gene was too diluted and became lost. Golden, Cream, and Cinnamon were the varieties most commonly seen. The Piebald, however, although of lively disposition, was inclined to be undersized.

Another spotted form, the **Dominant Spot**, has tended to replace the Piebald. There is the same variation in the amount of white on the body. Here too, the coloured areas may be either Golden, Cream Cinnamon, Blonde, etc., and it is necessary to speak of a Cream Dominant Spot, for instance, for a full description. Unlike the Piebald, Dominant Spot hamsters are not undersized and the females make excellent mothers.

The **Roan** hamster (see fig. 9) should have the appearance of a white body and a marbling of colour going down from the head in the form of even, heavy ticking. Roans are most often found in Sable, Cream and Mink but may also be produced in Yellow and Umbrous Smoke Pearl with selective breeding. Roan is produced by the White Bellied gene. Two animals bred using this gene should never be mated together as this can produce babies with small, rudimentary eyes or no eyes at all. This means that all Roans should be mated back to plain Creams, plain Sables or plain Minks, etc. Self animals from the Black gene rather than the Cream gene may be combined with the White Bellied gene which gives the animals a silvered appearance rather than a roaned one, with a covering of white guard hairs over the body.

White Band, Piebald, Dominant Spot and Roan

Fig. 9. Roan hamster.

are all "patterned" hamsters, so styled because they are primarily a colour variety, with a pattern of white superimposed.

Coat Varieties

The **Satin** is an interesting variety. It is the first of the coat variations to appear in the Syrian hamster. The colour is unchanged but the coat has a glossy appearance – hence the name. Furthermore, the colour is noticeably richer in the Satin. This can produce some remarkably beautiful animals. Two Satins should never be mated together, as a percentage of the litter will be born as Double Satin coated. These animals have very fine, greasy-looking fur and, although healthy, are not as attractive as normal hamsters. A Satin should always be mated to the normal coated equivalent colour.

The **Rex** (see fig. 10) is an intriguing variety. The coat is unique, being dense and slightly woolly to the touch. Young Rexes have a very wavy appearance, but this is less obvious in the adult. The guard hairs are curly and this is the reason for the rex coat. The whiskers are also curved, very different from the straight whiskers of the normal. When Rexes were first produced, their coats were initially very thin and fine. Through selective breeding, Rex hamsters nowadays have equally as plush fur as their normal coated counterparts.

The **Long-haired** (see fig. 11) is one of the most gorgeous varieties when in full coat. The coat is long and silky, especially for the male because of a pronounced sex difference between the sexes. The males

Fig. 10. Rex hamster.

have by far the longest coat. The full length of hair is usually not attained until six to eight months. There is a tendency for the coat to matt in older animals, so be prepared to disentangle gently any knots which may appear. Grooming is best done with the fingers at first, as this pulls less hair out. Then a final quick going over with a small, soft brush or toothbrush will tidy the coat up and add that extra sheen.

The various coat types may be found in any of the known colours. Thus it is possible to have Albino, Cinnamon, Cream, Grey Satin or Long Hair among others. It is also possible to have Satin Rex and/or Long Hair. The coat of the latter is extraordinarily fine.

Fig. 11. Male and female Long-haired hamster.

Exhibiting

One of the thrills of keeping hamsters is entering them in competition with others for prizes. First-class exhibition hamsters are usually superior to those bought at a pet store. Nevertheless, this fact need not deter anyone who wishes to exhibit from doing so. Some very good hamsters have been purchased from a pet shop. There is also another aspect. Many shows have special classes for junior exhibitors (under sixteen years of age), for Novices (those who have not won a first prize more than twice) and pet classes where the exhibit is judged in its own cage on its condition, health and friendliness rather than on show points. The existence of these classes gives the beginner a real chance of winning a prize since the "old hands" at showing cannot compete in the same classes.

Hamster shows are of two sorts. There are those put on by agricultural exhibitions, horticulture shows and local council fêtes. Many of these have livestock sections and the hamster may be included along with guinea-pigs, rabbits, mice, etc. The advantages of these shows are that they are conveniently near for visiting and that they cater for pets rather than for exhibition animals. Anyone desiring to show must first ascertain if there are classes for hamsters and obtain a copy of the show rules. These rules are usually quite simple and are to ensure that everything is above board and that entries are properly made.

The other types of shows are organised by hamster clubs. These may be devoted entirely to hamsters or be part of a larger show, of which hamsters are an important section. Hamster clubs occasionally do have official shows at local fêtes and agricultural shows too. A visit to one of these is much more exciting and rewarding than those previously mentioned. The quality of the exhibits would be expected to be higher and many of the varieties of hamster can be seen under one roof including several species of Dwarf hamsters. There is opportunity to meet people whose main interest is hamsters and who are interested enough to guide the footsteps of a beginner.

Taking Part in a Show

Details of shows in the UK are available from the clubs' secretaries. A schedule for each show will be sent in advance with the date, address, judges and classes listed. Pets may be entered on the day but the main show must be entered several days beforehand.

If you enter the main show, your hamster will have to be exhibited in an official show cage or "pen". Novices may hire show pens for the first year or two. At the show you should collect your pen label and a hired pen or two from the Show Secretary. Short-haired Syrians and Dwarfs should have a layer of wood shavings placed in the pens, whilst long-haired Syrians should be shown on wood-based cat litter.

All the hamsters are laid out in their classes, on tables forming a square or a U shape. The judge has a table in front of him/her, where the majority of the class to be assessed is put by a volunteer called a "pen steward". That way the judge can examine the whole class at a glance and see what kind of quality there is.

Bedding is not allowed in the show pen, only a small piece of fruit or vegetable and a dog biscuit. All the show pens are exactly the same size, colour and design. The only way to tell them apart is the label on the top, in the lefthand corner. This has your own personal number for that animal, plus all the classes that the hamster is entered in.

The pen steward's job is to organise the hamsters into numerical order, in class order. Then he brings the groups of hamsters to the judge as they are required. The judge has a personal secretary called the "book steward" who writes down all comments and scores. The pen stewards move the show pens along the tables as each class is judged, making space for the animals which have been judged already to go back in after the un-judged ones. After being judged, each pen label gets the total score written on. The pen steward must put the hamsters back in score order, which means the classes all get mixed up. This does not matter, as it is the score from the first class which is used to determine where the animals come in their next class. By the end of the show, all the hamsters are in score order with the best at the top and the worst at the bottom. The judge can then see at a glance what should be awarded Best In Show. People officiating in such a way get to hear the judge's comments and see things that the other exhibitors do not and it is a good way for them to gain experience towards becoming judges themselves.

The first hamster club was started in 1945 just after World War Two and was called the British Hamster Club. The formation of regional clubs happened soon after. Eventually the name changed and it became the National Hamster Council.

At the time of writing, the hamster is well served by a number of societies catering for both the Syrian and Dwarf species. Some are regional while others cover the whole country. Probably the most versatile is the British Hamster Association or BHA as it is often known. This club looks after the interests of all species. The BHA is the main organisation to which the local clubs are affiliated. It governs the show standards and publishes a wide range of pamphlets on the keeping of individual species and of their different varieties.

London and the southern counties have a regional body known as the Southern Hamster Club which was the first club to incorporate shows for Dwarf hamsters. The Heart of England Hamster Club is also for members based in the London area and the counties that are east, west and north of London, whereas the Midlands and northern counties have their own club too. This is known as The Hamster Society and is often abbreviated to Hamsoc.

Friendly rivalry exists between the clubs but they are loosely knit together for the setting of common standards of excellence for the different hamster varieties, arrangement of competitive exhibitions and other activities. Monthly newsletters are issued which publish details of impending shows and venues, as well as the latest developments in the world of hamster breeding, not forgetting readers' letters.

Should you wish to show (or even if you do not), membership of one of these clubs is well worthwhile. You will then obtain news of when and where shows are to be held. Which club you should join will depend on where you live. If you are uncertain, the secretary of any one will soon advise you. Membership is inexpensive (mostly to pay for the journal and postage) and reduced fees are paid by juniors (those under sixteen years). Meetings arranged by these clubs are more than just exhibitions. Members can get together to chat about their hobby, and ideas can be aired far better than in any amount of letter writing. If interested parties want to join a club and do not have details of their local one, the BHA may be contacted directly and details will be given of their most local club(s).

A standard show pen must be used for exhibiting at hamster club shows. This is necessary not only to aid the judge in his task but also to avoid any suggestion that it is possible to know who owns which exhibit. The pens can be made at home according to specifications laid down by the British Hamster Association. The specifications will be passed on to you when you join one of the clubs. Alternatively, new or second hand pens can often be bought quite cheaply through the hamster clubs.

It is rather obvious that no hamster should be considered for showing which is not in tip-top condition. It should be bright of eye, full of vigour and capable of being handled by strangers. Many a good hamster has failed on the show table because of unfriendly behaviour. The animal should also be perfectly clean and free from stains, particularly if it is light-coloured or white. Be sure to use fresh, white sawdust or preferably wood shavings for short-haired Syrian and Dwarf hamsters and wood-based cat litter for long-haired Syrians in the show pen and do not include food or liquid which could stain or mess the coat in any way. Pay attention to the show pen. There must be no distinguishing features nor should it be dirty. If it arrives back from a show scratched on the outside or the white paint on the inside has become yellowish, have it repainted in good time for the next show.

Whenever possible it is best to take hamsters to shows in special boxes, known as "travelling boxes". These are specially constructed containers built to hold the show pens comfortably and without shaking. Some may be purchased with lids but usually they do not have them.

It is often possible to examine travelling boxes at shows and you should be able to obtain hints on how to build one of your own. As with show pens, it is often possible to buy either new or second hand travelling boxes through the various hamster clubs. Most boxes are capable of holding four or six show pens and are also a convenient means of transporting hamsters by hand.

8

HEALTH PROBLEMS AND COMMON AILMENTS

Hamsters are hardy little fellows and, properly fed and caged, rarely suffer from disease. However, illness can occur even in the best of homes and it is wise to be aware of the various troubles which may arise. In this way it should be possible to take action while the disease is in its early stages.

The most general signs of illness in small animals are listless behaviour, loss of appetite and bedraggled coat. The animal obviously "feels" ill and miserable, ceases to look for food and makes scarcely any effort to keep its coat carefully groomed. This is very bad because small animals have little fat reserves and they cannot go without food for long. Their small size makes the giving of most sorts of medication more difficult than, for example, a cat or a dog. However, this does not mean that nothing can be done. The art of success is to rally the resources of the animal so that it can fight its way back to good health.

There are a number of general principles which should be followed in the treatment of disease.

The first and foremost is that the sickly hamster must be isolated from its fellows if you have several. This is a precaution in case the disease is infectious. It should be moved to another room and you should always tend to the healthy animals first. To move from the sick to the healthy is just asking for the disease to spread. Always wash your hands thoroughly after tending to the sick animal; use a mild germocide if you wish, but old-fashioned soap and water are almost as good if you use plenty of soap and rinse your hands well. None of these precautions is necessary, of course, for an injury or other non-infectious disease.

Warmth is always beneficial. The sick animal should be moved to a heated room. Whether or not this is possible, the little invalid could be placed in a box with a hot-water bottle. A baby's rubber hot-water bottle is ideal for a hamster (if this can be inserted into his usual cage, so much the better; a sick animal is not likely to gnaw it). In any event, the nest should be placed alongside it, together with extra soft bedding. Make sure that the animal is snug in its nest and that the warmth is reaching him. Test the warmth with your hand. If it is too hot for comfort, it is too hot for the hamster. Similarly, when the hot-water bottle has cooled, refill it immediately. Do not wait until the bottle is stone cold, obviously. Sick animals require rest, so do not disturb him unnecessarily. The warmth may revive the little fellow and, if you hear him moving, this is the occasion to tempt him with tasty morsels of food.

Wet-Tail

The most serious disease of hamsters is a severe form of diarrhoea known as "wet-tail". The symptoms are usually a yellow to mustard-coloured, very watery discharge which sometimes surrounds a solid area of faeces and can cover the whole vent area, including the base of the tail. The smell is quite offensive and pungent. Hamsters stop eating and drinking and lose condition within 24-48 hours. Their faces usually become drawn and pinched and they sit hunched with their eyes half closed. The onset of the disease is rapid. Recovery is rare despite all forms of treatment. The disease is very infectious. Veterinary treatment should be sought immediately and antibiotics and re-hydration treatment will be prescribed.

Before any thought is given to obtaining another hamster, all bedding and sawdust which have been in contact with the infected animal must be burned (or otherwise permanently disposed of). The cage, feeding pots and water bottles must be washed with a disinfectant which is deemed harmless for hamsters and thoroughly rinsed through afterwards.

Diarrhoea

Most cases of diarrhoea are not due to the dreaded "wet-tail" disease. Mild cases are not infrequent and usually arise from the hamster eating something which has disagreed with it. Soiled food is a common cause and this can be avoided in the main by regular cage cleaning. The feeding of unaccustomed food or too much green food or fruit could bring on the diarrhoea. There may also be some loss of condition, but recovery is almost certain so long as the animal retains its appetite. Stop feeding green food, fruits or roots immediately and allow the hamster only dry food and water. The normal diet can be resumed a few days after the diarrhoea has ceased.

For hygiene reasons, the cage should be cleaned out more regularly (daily, if possible), with frequent renewal of bedding. Hamsters can be peculiar in that certain foods upset some animals and not others. If certain foods do upset your hamster, you should not give them in the future.

Colds

Sniffy breathing, running noses and wheezing may be due to various causes. The most serious is an infectious "cold" which can distress the hamster by interfering with its breathing and producing a running nose. The symptoms can be relieved, if not cured, by keeping the invalid warm. The condition often clears spontaneously. If it does not, however, you may need to seek advice from a veterinarian who may prescribe a course of antibiotics.

Snuffles and running eyes may result from draughts or too dry an atmosphere. Take care not to have the cage over a hot radiator or the like. Irritants in the sawdust or hay can be troublesome on occasions. A good test of these materials is to try them on oneself. If a deep breath causes one's nose to tingle, they may be causing distress to the hamster. The offending material should be discarded.

Constipation

This is rather uncommon and the exact cause unknown. The stomach often appears swollen and the hamster moves around stiffly in a hunched position. Incorrect feeding is a likely cause and reinforces the advice to feed a varied diet at all times. Some green vegetables or a pinch of Epsom salts dissolved in the water bottle may be of help.

Injuries

Injuries may result from innumerable causes. Wounds arising from the animal catching itself on sharp edges of the cage or cage equipment are possible, although the coat gives surprisingly good protection in this respect. Accidents due to excitable play are a little more common. Falls also contribute their quota of cuts and bruises. Hamsters fall very awkwardly and they should be prevented from climbing into positions where a fall could be harmful. Fighting between animals can be vicious and nasty gashes can be opened up by their claws and teeth.

Treatment of wounds will depend on their seriousness. Slight wounds need no attention beyond that of checking that they do not turn septic. Hamsters are meticulous in their toilet and the continuous licking of the wound will keep it clean. Healing is usually rapid. Dressing would only irritate the animal and should not be attempted.

Hamsters with more serious wounds should be taken to a veterinary surgeon. Likewise, animals with broken limbs should be taken to a vet for attention. It is probable that these will mend of their own accord but it is wise to seek expert advice.

Falls

The hamster is quite an inquisitive creature and has no respect for heights. It has the unfortunate habit of peering over the edge of tables or shelves, inching forward until it is hanging by the hind legs. Sooner or later it will drop. The animal seems unable to land on its feet but falls heavily on its back, side or stomach. If the fall is a short one, the little chap is quickly on its feet.

Alas, if the fall is a long one, the breath is knocked from its body and it may lie there for a while slowly recovering. It may even be stunned. It is best to allow the hamster to recover of its own accord and not to attempt to hasten the process. Be warned, however, and do not allow your hamster to be unattended in situations where a fall could be disastrous.

Overgrown Teeth

The occasional animal may have teeth which are not worn down by the normal eating and gnawing activities. Giving the hamster baked husks of bread and "Bonio" dog biscuits may help, but not always. The main reason is that the teeth are not occluding properly. In time, these will interfere with feeding and should be clipped. You can do this yourself once shown how to, initially by a vet or someone else with experience.

Teeth can be clipped with teeth and nail clippers or small fine bladed wire cutters. The hamster should be scruffed tightly so that its mouth is held open and appears to be "smiling". Do not worry, even though they do not like it, it does not hurt and is a good way of immobilising them. This will reveal the two upper and two lower front teeth. The blades of the cutter should be placed around the overgrown tooth ensuring that the hamster's tongue is not too close and a quick action should snip off the offending length. Ideally the teeth should be 3-4mm long. If they split or crack along the length of the tooth, do not worry, just even off the stump with another careful cut.

If the remainder of the tooth falls out or starts to bleed a little, there is still no cause for concern. The blood will coagulate quickly and the missing tooth will grow back again within a few days. Hamsters feel little pain when having their teeth clipped. They are usually more upset and feel humiliated about being scruffed. Teeth cutting can be done as regularly as is necessary.

Long Claws
These may occur in extremely old hamsters. They may be trimmed with sharp scissors. Hold the foot up to the light and be careful only to trim the clear portion of the nail. Cutting too close to the toe could cause bleeding. Trimming should not be attempted unless the overgrown nails are causing distress. A vet will attend to the trimming if you do not wish to undertake it yourself.

Fleas and Mites

Neither of these pests should be a problem as a rule, if the cage is kept clean. Should they be suspected, the nest should be dusted with a flea powder or aerosol spray stated to be harmless for hamsters or cats. The insecticide will find its way into the coat. A little can be used directly on the animal if you can do this without upsetting him.

Tumours

Hamsters can suffer from cancers and tumours particularly with the onset of old age. These are often treatable and the hamster should be taken to a vet for diagnosis as soon as the owner becomes aware of any abnormalities on the skin.

Twisted Heads and Circling

There is a disorder of the inner ear which can sometimes affect the hamster's balance. As soon as a tilt of the head is apparent, or if the hamster starts to circle, it should be taken to a vet for advice. This could be due to an infection which may be treatable with antibiotics.

There is also an inherited condition, sometimes known as "waltzing", with similar symptoms which start to show when baby hamsters are around two weeks old. Often the hamster is completely incapable of walking in a straight line and may run around in circles until exhausted. This is more serious as there is no cure. It is usually best to have the hamster showing this condition humanely destroyed by a vet.

Cataracts and Blindness

Sometimes due to excessive cage bar chewing, a hamster can rub its eye so badly that a cataract forms. This is a milky looking layer over the surface of the eye-ball which reduces the animal's vision, sometimes completely. Usually not very much can be done to treat this. If the damage is not too serious, a vet may be able to prescribe eye-drops to help. Cataracts are not usually painful. If the cataract does not respond to treatment the hamster will be able to manage with the use of only one eye, as they have poor eyesight anyway and will rely more on the use of their whiskers to negotiate their way around.

Anophthalmic Hamsters (Eyeless Hamsters)

There is a gene in Syrian hamsters which can cause babies to be born with small, rudimentary eyes or no eyes at all. This is called the white bellied gene or anophthalmic white gene.

It is only when two white bellied animals are mated together that eyeless animals are born. If a white bellied animal is mated to a non white bellied animal, all of the litter will be healthy and have normal eyes. Approximately half the litter will be non white bellied and half the litter will be white bellied. A normal hamster from a white bellied parent cannot carry the gene. Therefore there is no worry that "carriers" will get together to produce eyeless young. If two white bellied hamsters are mated together, the ratio of young should be: 25% normal, 50% white bellied and 25% eyeless.

Eyeless hamsters will adapt to normal life, relying

on smell, sound and use of their whiskers to compensate. The layout of their cage should not, however, be changed too much. They should be treated and handled with more care than sighted animals until they become completely used to their owner.

Spinal Deformities

Dark Greys and colours bred from dark grey are particularly prone to mild spinal deformities. These are usually not so serious as to threaten the mobility of the hamster, but rather are seen in the form of a bent, kinked or shortened tail. Animals with such tails may not be shown and should not be bred from.

Thin Coat

The normally thick coat of the hamster may become thin in old animals, particularly on the stomach. This is quite natural and is only mentioned in case you should feel concerned. So long as the skin is not inflamed, there is nothing to be alarmed about. Brewer's yeast or dog conditioning tablets may be crushed up and sprinkled onto the dry food and may help to alleviate this. Should inflammation be present, it may be that the animal has developed a skin disease. If so, the hamster should be shown to a vet for his advice.

Hip Glands

The two hip glands of the hamster secrete an oily substance, and, on occasion, this may cause the fur around the glands to become "damp". Since the glands are normally hidden by the fur, their sudden prominence may worry some people. It is easy to think that the hamster has a couple of sore spots. However, this is unlikely and an occasional oily patch is natural.

Hibernation
This is not a disease but may be noted because of the distress the condition may cause to the hamster's owner. The little chap may appear lifeless – curled up, with his head pointing to his tail, cold and no obvious breathing. The condition used to be very common and brought on by low temperature. Nowadays it is rare for hamsters to hibernate even in very cold weather. Always provide plenty of bedding so that a warm nest can be built and hibernation will continue to be a thing of the past.

Should hibernation occur, however, it is essential to bring the animal out of it slowly. The hot-water bottle treatment described earlier is usually effective. Be sure to allow him to wake up naturally and he will soon be lively and running about. Once a hamster has hibernated, it means that it may do so again if the temperature falls. Keeping a cage in a warm room or in a room which has been warm for most of the day will help to prevent recurrences.

9

DWARF HAMSTERS: DIFFERENT SPECIES

Many of the Dwarf hamsters inhabit regions of north-east Russia, including Siberia, Mongolia, Manchuria, parts of northern China, central and eastern Asia, and eastern Kazakhstan, seemingly in the more semi-desert, scrub and steppe areas. Captive specimens were imported into Britain during the 1960s and 1970s for scientific study of their behaviour and breeding. Later small numbers were handed on to those breeders who were interested in exotic pets. The Dwarfs adapted very quickly in their new surroundings, adjusting to and thriving on life in captivity.

Among the various Dwarf hamsters, three species particularly have come to the fore in recent years. Each is popularly known as the Russian hamster. Although two are remarkably similar in appearance and size, they are distinct species. Breeders distinguish between these two sorts by the vernacular names of "Campbell's Hamster" (*Phodopus Sungoris Campbelli*) and "Winter White" (*Phodopus Sungoris Sungoris*). The third species is the Roborovski

Fig. 12. Campbell's Russian hamster.

Russian hamster (*Phodopus Roborovski*).

The Russian hamsters are among the smallest of the hamster group of species, truly living up to the name of Dwarf. They are about 5cm (2 inches) long or so when fully grown, the males being slightly but noticeably larger than the females. Both species have a scent gland on the belly which is especially obvious in the males. Campbell's, in particular, spread the scent over their bodies when grooming. A bowl of chinchilla dust placed in the cage for half an hour every few days makes an excellent grooming bath for Russian hamsters, and prevents them from becoming too greasy looking.

Of the two similar species, the Campbell hamster

Fig. 13. Winter White Russian hamster.

appears to be the most popular, possibly because they are the most easy to breed and are particularly fertile, although, of course, this could change at any time.

The Dwarf hamsters may rightly be described as cute. They may be appreciably smaller than the Syrian hamster, but they have a fascinating charm of their own. Unlike their larger cousin, more than one may be kept together. In fact, they seem by nature to be gregarious, small groups living quite contentedly with one another. This is by far the better way of keeping the little creatures and presents no problem because of their daintiness. If you have no wish to bother with breeding, ensure that the colony members consist entirely of the same sex. Either sex is suitable as excellent pets.

The coat is extraordinarily thick and luxuriant for such a small animal, which is suggestive that the natural habitat for the species is inclined to be cold, especially after nightfall. Even the feet are covered in hair, a feature which has given rise to the alternative name of "Hairy Footed Hamster". The wild colour of both species of Russian hamster is a medium shade of grey-brown, being more buffish-brown in the Campbell's hamster and more grey in the Winter White. They both have a conspicuous dark line along the spine, stretching from almost between the ears to the base of the tail. The stomach fur can be white or very pale buff grey. The tail is stubby, so much so that it is usually hidden by the dense fur.

The Campbell hamster retains the typical grey-brown colour throughout the year, whereas the Winter White may change colour to off-white during the autumn and winter months. This is the reason for the common name of the species. However, the colour change can be prevented by keeping the hamster in a "summer time" 24 hour cycle of artificial illumination of 16 hours light with eight hours darkness.

The Roborovski Russian hamster is the most recently introduced species to the British pet market. As described earlier, they are a light sandy gold colour with a white throat and eyebrows, a rather short face and no spinal stripe.

They seem to have even more energy than the Campbell's and Winter White Russian Dwarfs, seemingly constantly on the go. Roborovskis have a real spring in their step and can jump heights over six inches (15cm). As they are so small and move so rapidly, they are not suitable as children's pets. Great care is needed when handling, for if they get on to the floor they run extremely fast and are very difficult to catch. Despite this they seldom bite and are very healthy.

As, it seems, with all the species of Russian hamsters, if kept in a colony situation they are best suited to even numbers of animals within the group. With odd numbers, there is often one that gets picked on and bullied.

Less popular than the Russians, but still regularly seen in pet shops and at hamster shows is the Chinese hamster (see fig. 14). Perhaps this is because the shape of the body is longer and the tail is more obvious and mouse-like or maybe because they are so reclusive and like to hide away under bedding and cage litter. Nonetheless, they are very friendly and, once used to being handled, enjoy being petted. They are often known to sit in the palm of the hand or on the shoulder, quietly surveying what is going on around them.

Fig. 14. Chinese hamster.

10

DWARF HAMSTERS: HOUSING AND FEEDING

Housing and feeding requirements for Dwarf hamsters are very similar to those recommended for the Syrian hamster. They may be kept in identical cages, so long as the bars are not so wide apart that the little animal can squeeze between them. This is a point to watch if you are thinking of a cage. If baby Dwarf hamsters come along they can get through the tiniest of gaps. Dwarf hamsters are little digging machines and will also make a lot of mess unless a cage tidy is put around the whole cage (see Chapter 4, page 35). However, many people have found that medium to large glass aquarium tanks are eminently more suitable for Dwarfs.

The advantage of aquaria is that the clear glass permits an unobstructed view of the antics of the inmates. This is an important aspect of keeping the Dwarf species for, strictly speaking, they are to be observed rather than handled. Their little bodies are not robust enough to withstand accidental rough treatment. In the Campbell's Russian, some individuals of both sexes are prone to nip if not handled carefully. Breeders are advised to do all that they can to breed out this tendency.

The aquaria should be spacious because the Dwarfs are lively, quick in action, and extremely inquisitive. Their "busy-body" behaviour is charming to watch. Clean, dry and white wood-shavings for preference should be used as litter, this being removed as soon as it becomes wet or discoloured. Fresh hay, fine woodwool or plain paper from a kitchen roll may be given for bedding material. The latter may be inserted tightly screwed up, for the hamsters love to shred the material to construct their nests. Ample "toys" should be provided in the form of small cardboard tubes, branches from non-poisonous trees, or cardboard cartons. The animals will enjoy investigating these and chewing them to pieces. The customised glass tanks that are available in some pet shops, which have ramps, ledges and ladders round the walls, really keep the inhabitants' minds and bodies stimulated. It is most entertaining to watch individuals in small colonies, scurrying from level to level.

Transparent plastic storage boxes with wire mesh lids also make good homes for Dwarf hamsters. These are quite cheap and if they become too badly scratched with wear can be replaced for little expense.

Should any of these little fellows escape, you could try using the deep-sided trap method to catch them as described on page 29, Chapter 3. Alternatively there is a humane mouse trap which catches very small animals alive and is very effective for getting these little pets back safely. This consists of a rectangular box tube with a trip mechanism which releases a trap door when the floor halfway inside is trodden on. If you do lose a Dwarf and set one of these traps you must check it every few hours, for if the animal is left inside for too long it could dehydrate.

The Dwarfs are essentially grain eaters, relishing almost all types of cereals and pulses. These may be fed either in a natural state, as mixed grains, or as processed pellets, biscuits or dried cake and bread. Stale bred may be fed as such, or baked dry (in small cubes) in an oven. Small amounts of fresh food in the form of leaves, roots and fruit may be given, as advised for the Syrian hamster. Rather like their bigger cousins, they do not appear to be fussy eaters, consuming almost anything we humans can eat, provided it is wholesome. Fresh water should be available at all times, preferably in the form of an automatic watering bottle.

Two cheek pouches are present and these are used but they do not seem to be as extensive as those of the Syrian hamster, even allowing for the small size of Dwarfs.

11

DWARF HAMSTERS: BREEDING

Breeding presents scarcely any problems with the Dwarfs. The most successful methods of breeding are either as a pair (male and female) or as a trio. Larger groups or colonies of mixed sexes may be kept together, but this is unwise because litters will be born of different ages and the babies of the younger ones are likely to be trampled underfoot.

It is recommended that Winter Whites should only be bred from in pairs. They really do not fare well in colony situations. Dominant males may harass, bully and even kill the lower ranking males in the group and the dominant female is likely to do the same to both lower ranking males and females. Jealousies happen in trio situations as well, and one individual may turn on the others even after the three hamsters may have lived in harmony for months and even raised several litters together. Male and female Winter Whites in pairs, once bonded, rarely squabble if given enough living space.

There are not usually serious problems with colonies of Campbell's Russians as long as one sex is not in too great a majority.

With Chinese hamsters, the females are the most aggressive. They will do well in pairs, or trios with two males and one female, or even colonies with one female and up to six males. Never keep sexually mature females together if they are with males as they are very likely to attack each other and injure the males, especially when they are in season or preparing to give birth to a litter. Unmated Chinese hamster females tolerate each other much better and are less likely to injure one another.

Selected individuals should be placed together before they attain sexual maturity at about 12-15 weeks of age. If a female has a litter before this age, do not worry, as nature has ensured that she is capable of rearing a litter so early. The gestation period is usually around 21 days and the typical litter is four to five babies. These are born naked, pink and with closed eyes. The skin darkens at the third day of life and hairs appear at between six to seven days.

If a mother dies and another female has a litter of a similar age, Dwarf hamsters make wonderful foster mothers. I have known a Chinese with six one-week-old babies, feed and raise seven other babies from another female as well as her own. The young from the dead female were gently rolled around in the sawdust from the new cage then mixed into the nest with the existing babies whilst the foster mother was distracted with some food. She then returned to the nest a few moments later and took over mothering her extra charges.

The eyelids open about fourteen days. At this stage the young will be moving about and seeking food. They will exhibit a fierce twittering sound if disturbed. By three weeks, the young Dwarfs are capable of fending for themselves.

Sexing can be a problem in young animals, but can be determined by the distance between the anus and the urinary pimple. These are very close in the female, almost touching, but with space between them in the male.

The babies are like miniature adults at this age. They should be weaned promptly because another litter is likely to be due at any time. In common with many other rodent species, the females are mated shortly after they have given birth. Litters from different mothers usually end up in the same nest and are tended by both. This is quite satisfactory provided they do not differ in age by more than a week or so. It is intriguing that the male will snuggle up with the mother(s) and litter, helping to keep the babies warm. If males and females are left together, the female of all the Dwarf species commonly kept as pets will have several litters in continuous succession. This could be at any time of the year. The Roborovski females, however, are different in the fact that they are seasonal breeders and may not actually produce their first family until nearly a year old. This would be at a time when most other Dwarfs are nearing the end of their fertile period. Once started, the Roborovski may have three or four litters in a row about three or four weeks apart.

It may be mentioned that the two similar-looking Russian Dwarfs (Campbell's and Winter Whites) are true species. Numerous attempts have been

made to cross the species but apparently with nega-
tive results. This is a sign of authentic speciation
since true species do not inter-mate or, if they do,
the offspring either die at an early age in the womb
or are sterile.

12

DWARF HAMSTERS: VARIETIES AND EXHIBITING

Shows for the Dwarfs are usually held in conjunction with those for the Syrian hamster, if only for the reason that many people keep and breed both forms. At one time, only the wild-coloured grey-brown was to be seen, but there are now more and more colourful varieties and different coat types. Until the mid 1980s only Syrian hamsters were shown to a standard. Nowadays at all shows there are classes for each species of Dwarf hamster except the Roborovski which is too lively and too quick to be judged at present.

The Campbell's Russian Dwarf (*Phodopus Sungoris Campbelli*)

Colours
The Campbell can boast of the **Albino**, a variety with a snowy white coat, flesh-coloured ears and pink eyes. It was discovered in 1988.

A very pretty colour is the **Argente**. The top coat is

a light sandy beige, with a fine, darker brown-grey line down the middle of the back. The under-colour is blue grey. The eyes are a rich ruby red and the ears are flesh-coloured. This variety was imported to the United Kingdom in 1993. It has been reported that there is a Black-eyed form of the Argente overseas, yet to be brought into the UK.

The **Black** Campbell's Russian arrived in the UK from Europe in 1998. They can vary from a very dark all over self black to a grey-black with a visible darker stripe showing through. The Black has been responsible for several new variations, one of which is the Dove Campbell. The **Dove** is a self brown colour, rather more chocolate in colour than the Dove Syrian hamster. It is a combination of Argente and Black. It has dark red eyes.

A very attractive variety is the **Black-eyed White** which is pure white as the name implies with jet-black, large, beady eyes. This variety often has dark or patched ears.

A most unusual colour is the **Opal**, which is a smoky-blue colour with a dark grey stripe and black eyes.

The **Mottled** variety has white markings on the head and body. These may vary from small spots to quite extensive areas. The former are often called Spotted, while the latter are regarded as the true Mottled. The variety may be bred in all the existing colours, the Black and White Mottleds having the greatest contrast in colour and being particularly striking to look at.

There is another white patterning gene in the Campbell hamster. This is the **Platinum**. Whereas

Mottleds have definite patches of white, Platinums have streaks of white guard hairs running through the coat across the back, shoulders and flanks. The amount of white guard hairs increases as the animal matures until some hamsters are almost pure white. Platinums may also be found in all the existing colours and especially make Blacks look "silvery". When two Platinums are bred together, the result can be a very diluted colour. Normal Platinums bred together will produce Black-eyed Whites. Argente Platinums bred together will give a pure white animal with red eyes which looks very similar to the Albino.

Coat Types

Two coat variations other than normal have also made an appearance. The first is in the form of Satin. The coat is finer than the normal and displays a satiny gloss. Satins may be bred in any of the above colours. The second is the Rex which first appeared in Bedfordshire in 1996. Like the Rex Syrian hamster, the coat is curly and seems shorter than normal fur. The whiskers also look crimped. Rexes may be produced in all of the above colours.

The Winter White Russian Dwarf *(Phodopus Sungoris Sungoris)*

Three colour varieties are known for the Winter White aside from the normal wild agouti colour. A very attractive one is the **Pearl,** being white all over and covered in grey ticking all over the body, complete with a spinal stripe. As the animal matures, the ticking fades until an almost white animal is left.

The aptly named **Sapphire** is a bluish grey in colour, again with a slightly darker spinal stripe.

The third colour is a combination of the above two, the **Sapphire Pearl**. The coloured ticking is paler than the ordinary Pearl, with a light bluish blush to the coat. The eyes are dark in all of the varieties. At present there is only one coat type in this species.

The Chinese Hamster *(Cricetulus Griseus)*
Chinese hamsters are found in a spotted form as well as the normal grey-brown colour. Black-eyed Whites are produced on very rare occasions. It would appear that they are over-spotted with no colour on them. They do not seem to be able to reproduce further pure white offspring, only normal and spotted.

13

DWARF HAMSTERS: COMMON AILMENTS

In principle, the Dwarfs could suffer from all the ailments which could strike the Syrian hamster, but, fortunately this does not seem to be the case. Provided they are housed sensibly and fed a varied and adequate diet, they have few illnesses.

Diarrhoea
Diarrhoea may be a problem and can usually be traced to incorrect feeding. An afflicted animal should be immediately isolated from its companions (if in a colony) and tempted to eat with tasty tit-bits.

Water should not be withheld, for, contrary to what is sometimes a common belief, water as such is not a cause of diarrhoea.

The prompt removal of the afflicted hamster is advisable because severe diarrhoea could be due to an infectious agent which could affect all of the colony. It follows that all cages or aquaria which have housed an affected animal should be cleansed with suitable disinfectant before re-use.

Diabetes

Diabetes may be found in any species of hamster and is occasionally present in the Campbell. As the dosage of insulin required for a hamster would be too small to administer, the hamster therefore cannot be treated for this.

One finds that the hamster drinks two or three times his normal amount of water. This means that cage cleaning must be done more frequently.

A hamster with a mild case of diabetes may live as long as a healthy one, but sadly this is not usually the case. One can only ensure that the animal's quality of life is as good as possible and, when the hamster visibly seems to decline, then a trip to the vet would be necessary to end the suffering humanely.

Glaucoma

Glaucoma, a swelling of the eyeball, is another problem occasionally suffered by the Campbell. As long as the eye does not look uncomfortably large, the hamster should not feel any discomfort. This is also not a treatable condition. Obviously any animals with signs of Glaucoma or diabetes should not be bred from.

Injuries

The rough and tumble of playful fighting may cause minor injuries. However this is rare, probably due to the thick protective coat of the little animals but also because playfulness seems to be part of their life and is rarely vicious. Any individual with an injury or wound which becomes infected should be taken to a vet for treatment.

Fleas and Mites

Unwanted visitors in the form of fleas and mites appear to be non existent but, if these are suspected, a dusting with a flea powder or spray which is safe for hamsters will quickly eliminate them. Do not forget to sprinkle a small quantity in the nest since this is the usual haunt for eggs of these parasites.

INDEX

FREE